Music Educators National Conference

MUSIC FACILITIES:
BUILDING, EQUIPPING, AND RENOVATING

By Harold P. Geerdes

To my wife, Gladys, without whose sympathetic support and understanding this volume would never have come into being.

Harold P. Geerdes is associate professor of music emeritus at Calvin College, Grand Rapids, Michigan. A longtime music educator and MENC member, he also has been active as a music facility planner and acoustician since 1970. He appears regularly at MENC regional and national conferences and is chairman of the MENC Committee on Music Rooms, Buildings, and Equipment. He is also author of the 1975 edition of Planning and Equipping Educational Music Facilities, *which has been widely used throughout the United States and Canada both as a planning guide and in college and university classes for future music teachers.*

William A. Stevenson of the Grand Rapids, Michigan, architectural firm of Daverman Associates used his good offices as chairman of the committee on Architecture for Education of the American Institute of Architects to secure photographs and drawings from a number of architectural firms across the country that are included in this book. Our appreciation is extended to him and to his colleagues.

CONTENTS

PREFACE TO THE 1975 EDITION

For many years, the Music Educators National Conference has recognized the importance of proper housing and good equipment for the efficient and effective teaching of music. This is the sixth publication of MENC devoted exclusively to this important subject. It is a revision and updating of the 1966 book, which (like its predecessors) was entitled *Music Buildings, Rooms and Equipment*. In 1932, the Music Education Research Council issued Bulletin No. 17, which was revised in 1938 and rewritten in 1949 and again in 1955. The 1966 edition received wide distribution and was used extensively during a period when many new music facilities were erected. Not all the music suites and auditoriums were equally successful. The need became apparent for a more extensive edition of the book with more attention to step-by-step planning procedures, technical aspects, and specialized requirements of music spaces. This book is an attempt to meet that need.

The author wishes to acknowledge the use of material, in some cases extensive, from the 1966 edition. Alteration and expansion of this material was undertaken only when that seemed essential, and certain sections are retained much as they appeared in 1966. The present edition benefits from a close collaboration with R. Lawrence Kirkegaard, manager of the Architectural Technologies Division of the Chicago office of Bolt, Beranek & Newman, who carefully reviewed early drafts of the manuscript.

A major contribution was made by Russell Johnson and his firm, Artec Consultants, New York City. His acoustical work on the Calvin College Fine Arts Center as a member of the Bolt, Beranek & Newman firm was so successful that the author was motivated to spend a sabbatical year with them and to share the knowledge and background gained by writing this book. Mr. Johnson was consulted often, and his advice and review of various drafts of the manuscript proved to be invaluable, as were the drawings he provided here. The section on illumination and color found in chapter four was updated by C. Harold Barcus, professor of architecture at Miami University, Oxford, Ohio, who also contributed this material to the 1966 edition.

Acknowledgment also is made to the following consultants for their assistance with various aspects of this publication: David Klepper and Gerald Marshall, Klepper, Marshall, King Associates, White Plains, New York; Jerry L. Monson, the Wenger Corporation, Owatonna, Minnesota; and Robert W. Wolff, Russell Johnson Associates, New York. MENC is also grateful to all of the schools, colleges, and architects who submitted photographs and drawings, of which only a small portion could be included here.

FOREWORD

The original 1975 edition of *Planning and Equipping Educational Music Facilities* was intended primarily as a guide to building and furnishing new structures. This revision has been published to update the original volume and is intended to help the many music teachers who can participate in the planning and construction of a new building, the renovation or conversion of existing spaces, or must make the most of what is available.

The spaces in which you teach music are extensions of the instruments and voices and are worthy of the concern and attention given to your instructional program.

Good music facilities have a convenient layout with adequate spaces for the full range of music instruction. Adequate means not only a space that is large enough and has desirable ceiling heights, but also one that has good acoustics, bright and noise-free lighting, proper and quiet ventilation, and good noise containment. Criteria detailed in this publication should be applied in each of these special areas. Spaces that fall short in any category should be considered liabilities to the program, since they do not properly support the activities carried on within them. Every effort should be made to convert these liabilities into assets.

Although a fine music suite does not guarantee a quality program, it certainly facilitates the work and reduces stress on both teachers and pupils. No other department has to make do with what is available as often as the music department. And often new facilities are not planned with the care and special expertise required to make them work well. This book is designed to help teachers plan new facilities and to overcome shortcomings in old ones. But the prescriptions given here cannot guarantee success without the help of an experienced practitioner in planning, acoustics, and noise control. Fortunately, such help is readily available if the busy music teacher will simply take the time to search it out.

INTRODUCTION

New approaches to education are reflected in changing concepts in the design of school buildings. These approaches have underscored the importance of providing specialized facilities to meet the needs of certain subjects like music. New technology and materials in themselves have not proven to be panaceas for the space and equipment problems that beset many music teachers. However, the knowledge and experience accumulated through the school building boom of recent decades have clarified these needs and have made apparent the need to stress the special requirements of areas devoted to music teaching. The days of assigning a music class or ensemble to any available space are, thank goodness, long past.

The waste of time and energy and the diminished productivity resulting from poor facilities cannot be justified at a time when spiraling costs and increasing demands on the educational system place a high premium on effective teaching and accountability. Adjusting or compromising a school music program to fit inadequate facilities is not an acceptable approach. To plan these facilities as though the schoolhouse exists in isolation from the community also is very shortsighted. Expanded adult education programs and increasing community use during nonschool hours make careful planning for such use imperative.

New buildings often have given music educators and school administrators a second chance. Unfortunately, many new facilities that do not work well for music also have been built. In the past, rather casual planning has been done mostly by an architect after briefing by the superintendent. This no longer is acceptable. A more viable approach involves team planning by the eventual users and designers with much interplay between them. Technical requirements for sound isolation, good room acoustics, and other functional capabilities are not left to chance, but are determined carefully by specialists working with a design team.

New approaches to teaching music may make new demands on traditional spaces. Electronic developments, with their varied implications for music education, must be accommodated. Wise and careful planning is needed to provide the optimum in equipment and the best possible facilities. Perhaps even more so than in some other subject areas, the proper tools and a hospitable environment will do much to enrich the teaching of music.

Music Facilities: Building, Equipping, and Renovating is intended to provide guidelines for the music educator, the administrator, the board of education, and the architect in designing and constructing new buildings or remodeling existing ones. It is broad in scope and it deals with music facilities at all levels: primary, secondary, and university. It is concerned with the location, design, and size of the facilities; storage and auxiliary space provided; auditoriums and music shells; and equipment placed in those facilities. In addition, it contains sample floor plans and photographs of recently completed facilities, and a bibliography of additional references.

The purposes of this publication are:

1. To guide the thinking of the music educator with regard to the physical requirements that are necessary for the successful performance of his or her duties.

2. To further acquaint the administrator and architect with some of the specialized departmental needs with which they may be only generally familiar.

3. To suggest proven, satisfactory approaches to some of the problems that commonly arise in the design and construction of new music facilities.

4. To provide a checklist of details to be considered in planning and furnishing the facilities so the music instructor can be confident that the music room is properly located, contains adequate storage areas, has adequate room acoustics and good sound isolation, and is not encumbered by other serious flaws that could have been corrected if attended to in time.

5. To arm the music educator with the facts and information needed to substantiate a presentation to the administration and the architect.

Music Facilities: Building, Equipping, and Renovating can be used by the music educator in the following ways:

1. He may familiarize himself with this material before preliminary discussions are begun in order to be more knowledgeable and better able to discuss the problems intelligently.

2. If he wishes to study certain areas in greater depth, he may consult the bibliography of additional references. Many of the titles include references to other materials that also may be helpful.

3. He can make this publication available to the administrator, architect, board of education, and other responsible persons.

4. He may review pertinent sections of this publication as planning and construction progress.

5. He may use this material to evaluate existing facilities to see if departmental needs are being met as adequately as possible in the space available. He may gain ideas for improving the present space. He may be encouraged to accept his present facilities not as an inescapable handicap, but to seek ways to make them work better for the music program.

A word of caution is in order. The "cookbook" approach with pat recipes to meet every need is a dangerous substitute for experienced consultants in any of the special areas of a music building. Advances in technology as well as improvements in music programs have combined to make these experts more important than ever.

CHAPTER 1

PLANNING MUSIC FACILITIES

Before effective planning can take place, there must a consensus regarding the community's basic educational philosophy and the nature and extent of the curriculum that arises from that philosophy. No single solution or set of solutions is ideal in every situation. A physical plant can successfully meet the needs of a community only when it is designed in terms of that community's particular educational philosophy and when it provides sufficient flexibility to accommodate reasonable modifications. The need for a strong, balanced music program must be demonstrated logically and convincingly by the music educator. When this is done, there will be far fewer difficulties securing the facilities needed to carry on the program.

Music educators must have an important voice in designing the music facilities. It is essential that they be consulted early in the planning stages and that their opinions be sought periodically thereafter. As the people who actually will be using the space and equipment, they are in a position to offer valuable practical advice. The school administration and the architect have an obligation to seriously consider suggestions contributed by the entire professional staff.

Music departments and music schools differ widely in the amount of attention devoted to each type of instruction (such as classes, private lessons, and ensemble rehearsals), and no architect can plan intelligently unless he or she is aware of the client's particular needs. As a first step in planning, therefore, the instructional program must be outlined for the architect. As planning continues, the relationship of the school's music program to that of the entire community must be explored. After-hours use by community music agencies is increasingly common. Adult education programs often offer music. Activities that keep the music suite busy into the evening hours are meeting with growing favor by educational facility planners. In some communities, it is only by establishing the needs of such full-time programs that new buildings can be sold to a constituency that often resists higher taxes. School bond issues are more likely to be approved when taxpayers can envision the larger benefits that will be available to them through a community center.

Just as the architect and administrator must be aware of the needs and problems of the music educator, the music educator must in turn be aware of their needs. Teachers need not hesitate to ask for the equipment and facilities that are necessary for the satisfactory performance of their duties, but they must be realistic in their requests. They must be able to justify their needs in terms of the philosophy of the institution. Furthermore, they must understand that the administration, which is subject to pressures from many sources, must reconcile the divergent interests of all parties (including the taxpayers).

The music educator and administrator share the responsibility for making certain that the facilities are adequate for the future needs of the school. Not only must they anticipate increases in student and faculty personnel, but they must consider changes in the nature or scope of the music curriculum. It is important to provide for full use of sophisticated instructional media. These aids promise far greater efficiency and flexibility in teaching than was previously possible.

During preliminary discussions, the music teacher should visit the music facilities of a new school nearby and talk with teachers who have used the facilities to find out what features they like or dislike. Occasionally, there is some discrepancy between the theoretical usefulness of a feature and its actual value. The teacher should be concerned with the reasons for his colleagues' preferences, since some of those reasons may or may not be applicable to his own circumstances. Whenever possible, the concepts of multi-use and flexibility should be explored and applied carefully. While compromises that might jeopardize the program must be avoided, there are many ways to maximize the use of facilities by careful planning. But being "flexible" should not be construed to mean "compromised."

PLANNING AND DESIGN TEAM

Even in schools with flexible space modules, music spaces tend to be inflexible and permanent. Planning, therefore, must be complete and accurate from the beginning. There will be little opportunity later to correct oversights or errors. The architect and administrator should add to the planning and design team an appropriate number of future users from both school and community. The team also should include consultants in special areas, such as acoustics, sound isolation, lighting, and auditorium design.

The planning and design team must be charged with real responsibilities and must take an active role with involvement by all members. Its work must be given high priority, and a record of all its deliberations must be kept. The team's recommendations must be written in a form that will serve as a basis for the architect's preliminary design sketches. These sketches should be reviewed carefully and made the subject of a report to the administration. The team has an important role to play in the planning process, and the experience, expertise, and understanding of each member should be used.

The Calvin College Fine Arts Center, Grand Rapids, Michigan is located on the Knollcrest Campus adjacent to a major public road with convenient parking to accommodate community access for concerts, dramas, and many other noncollege uses. Architects: The Perkins & Will Partnership, Daverman Associates.

STEPS IN PLANNING

The planning and design team should follow each of these steps when planning a music facility:

- The planned uses and requirements of each space should be programmed and be as detailed as possible.
- The preliminary design should be developed by the architect and planning consultant, based on the program details.
- After a careful review of the preliminary design, the architects must work on final schematic refinement and design.
- Planners should receive construction documents and details of specifications such as blueprints and a specifications book.
- The construction should be supervised frequently by someone sensitive to the special requirements of a music building.
- The consultants and specialists should carefully check all of the details and systems before final acceptance.

ORGANIZATION

No two projects are exactly alike and, of course, the previous general steps in planning cannot apply to every situation. The following items may apply to the planning for a larger building of which the music area is only a part; or, if it is a separate facility, they can stand by themselves. Each step is important—not one should be left out. They are based on the assumption that an architect has been retained and the administration is going to assemble a design team. The administration should:

1. Designate representatives of the school board or administration, music department, drama department, and others who share in using common areas to be on the planning and design team.

2. Review the educational goals and the activities that will be conducted to achieve those goals, develop a program for the facility, estimate space needs, and establish a preliminary budget.

3. Proceed with the schematic design: Review and refine it until it is satisfactory, get a cost estimate, incorporate the systems concepts (space design, sound system functions, and the like) that evolve out of the detailed information channeled from the user group, and research physical requirements, such as systems requiring conduit or other special provisions.

4. Proceed to the construction drawings with complete structural, mechanical, and electrical details, including sound and other electronic systems. Toward this end, determine the location of all fixed equipment and the necessary wiring.

5. Make provisions for detailed supervision of the construction so that all the special requirements (especially those relating to sound isolation, noise control, and acoustics) are adhered to strictly. Pay critical attention to airtight construction that will prevent sound from leaking to adjacent rooms.

6. Follow through and performance test all spaces, systems, and equipment. Orient the users and teach them how to take maximum advantage of the new facilities and equipment.

THE ROLE OF THE MUSIC EDUCATOR

The architect will appreciate answers to several basic questions:

What activities are involved? The architect, like most laypeople, does not know exactly what music educators do in their facilities. He or she may not even be sure of what questions are to be asked. He needs to be told the nature of the teacher's activities, such as rehearsing a band, teaching a general music class, coaching an ensemble, instructing a beginning string class, showing a film, or giving a private lesson.

How many pupils are involved? In addition to the expected enrollment of each class or performing group for each teacher, the architect will need to know the anticipated growth for the next five to ten years. For some classes or organizations, he may want to know the maximum effective size of such a group.

How do the activities fit into the total school program? A good building is planned for the program it houses. Thus, music teachers must remember the need for a large assembly area where they expose the entire student body to musical experiences.[1] They also should remember that by sharing music rooms with other classes (and thus combining available funds), they might be able to afford better quality construction.

Experience has shown that planning done under time pressures is likely to be faulty, incomplete, or uneconomical. As much lead time as possible should be provided so that faculty members' ideas can be reviewed and assimilated before they are presented to the architect. Because of the nature and variety of music learning experiences, the planning team must have acoustics and sound isolation in mind from the start. In the early stages of gathering ideas, it is essential to consider the implications for sound isolation and acoustics in each of the major areas: classrooms, private studios, practice rooms, large rehearsal rooms, concert facilities, offices, theory and listening laboratories, libraries, and storage areas. At this stage, it is desirable to anticipate future needs liberally, keeping in mind the institution's projected enrollment figures.

The size of the school or community is not always an adequate indication of the size of the music department or of its facility requirements. Schools in small communities or collegiate institutions may employ large music staffs and may offer both extensive and intensive music programs. Other schools may employ only one music specialist to do both the vocal and instrumental teaching. The institution's basic philosophy has an important influence on decisions that are made about music facilities. Once the nature of the program has been established, a primary factor in determining the needs of the music department is the number of teachers employed by the school for music activities. This number is more significant than simple school enrollment or area population.

If a new building is replacing an old one, the number and size of classrooms can be estimated by examining the existing facility. Allowances must be made for changes if existing rooms are too small or too large for needed additions. Projected changes in the department's program or method of operation (such as small lecture section being replaced by a large section or a related arts course being added to the department's program) will need to be considered. The demands that might be made on the facilities by departments other than music must not be overlooked.

When a new building is added or a new program is developed, existing institutions with comparable curricular offerings and enrollment should be visited to help establish a planning base. In the interest of economy, it will be necessary to consider whether large ensemble rooms or the recital hall can be used as classrooms for part of the day and if teaching studios and small ensemble practice rooms can also accommodate small classes or seminars.

Just as it is necessary to answer questions about educational purposes before making decisions related to instructional areas, it also is important to inquire about traffic patterns as they will affect the function of auxiliary areas. This is especially important for planning band, choir, and orchestra rehearsal rooms. With the large numbers of students involved and the complex movement necessary to pick up music and an instrument and find a seat, smooth traffic flow helps guarantee an orderly entry and time savings before a rehearsal can begin. Taking the preliminary sketches and following a typical student into and out of different areas is helpful in determining a good traffic pattern.

---

1. Karl D. Ernst and Charles L. Gary, eds., *Music in General Education* (Washington, D.C.: Music Educators National Conference, 1965), 10–11.

Asking questions such as the following will also be helpful:

- Before each rehearsal, will students pass through the instrument storage room to check out their instruments?
- Are folios picked up and returned to the music library at each rehearsal?
- Will students need to get their instruments or folios from storage areas while another rehearsal is in progress?
- Are uniforms and equipment distributed from the storage rooms, or is the area used only for dead storage during the summer?
- Will there be drinking fountains? To avoid congestion, should they be placed inside or outside the rehearsal room?

Answers to these and similar questions will influence the planning of such auxiliary area details as relative locations, size, and number of doors.

PLANNING CHECKLISTS

Although the roles that the administrator, music staff, and architect should play in an ideal collaboration have been explained above, the following checklists will guide each of these as they initiate their work.

General concerns

- Has a philosophy of music education been developed?
- Does this philosophy reflect the latest ideas in music in order to build for the future?
- Do all involved parties understand their role in the music education program?
- Have all concerned parties been given the opportunity to request facilities that will enhance teaching in their specific areas?
- Is provision being made for a manager to oversee the building operation and ensure its optimum use?
- Has a schedule of activities for the building been outlined?
- How could future growth affect the requirements of the building?

Specific concerns

For the administrator:

- Are the music teachers actively involved in the planning?
- Has the music staff drawn up projected enrollment figures for at least a five-year period?
- Has both the administration and the music staff considered the implications of community involvement in music activities?

For the music educator:

- Has the music program been coordinated with the drama department or other groups who might share the auditorium and its support spaces?
- Has the architect been given any special requirements in regard to acoustics, lighting, location, heating, humidity control, and so forth, that are necessary to the program?
- What new equipment will be needed to make the new facility functional?
- Do the teachers fully understand their roles in the program of music education?
- Have the teachers been given the opportunity to request facilities that will make it possible for them to do their best teaching?
- Has the architect been given the best estimates of the numbers of people involved in each phase of the music program?
- What are the possible changes for the music program in the future?

For the architect:

- Visit other schools with a music program similar to that desired in the school being planned.

- Meet with the music staff to find out what they want to do in their teaching, discuss the basic program, and design and review schematics.
- Visit classes and attend rehearsals and performances in order to be aware of their particular needs.
- Be familiar with the special engineering and design problems of acoustics, sound transmission, lighting, auditorium seating and sight lines, stage rigging and lighting, traffic control, temperature and humidity control, and other special elements associated with music teaching and performance, and call in a consultant to help with those areas that are not familiar.
- Consider the flexibility of facilities as the curriculum and the teachers' roles change and as community use of the facilities expands.
- Suggest new ways that the facilities can assist the music staff in reaching their objectives.

BUILDING CODES AND FIRE SAFETY REGULATIONS

Local and national building codes, safety guidelines and codes, and federal accessibility standards for the handicapped play a strong part in the planning and designing of all buildings but particularly those involving places of public assembly. It is the responsibility of the design team and the architect to research and comply with these various governmental requirements.

LOCATION OF THE MUSIC SUITE

A major consideration in planning music facilities is the location of the rooms, offices, and rehearsal areas. Many factors are involved, including the relationship of the various music areas to each other as well as to other parts of the school and the site itself.

Desirable locations

The location of music facilities in relation to the rest of the campus must be decided bearing in mind the convenience of movement for both students and equipment. There are distinct advantages to having the instrumental rehearsal hall near and on the same level as the auditorium. However, insisting on locating everything adjacent to the auditorium can create serious isolation problems. Although a corridor or storage area between the rehearsal hall and the stage can help provide sound isolation, sound locks with double sets of doors and a vestibule between them as well as isolation joints in floors and walls may be required. Special attention must be given to avoid a common wall between rehearsal rooms and the performance areas. Second- or third-floor locations should be avoided for instrumental rehearsal rooms unless a service elevator is provided for the heavy instruments and equipment and unless expensive sound isolation construction is specified. The music unit should have a direct outside entrance near the parking lot. A loading dock near the stage and music suite should be easily accessible from either the street or driveway. An outside entrance to the drill field is advisable for marching bands. The music suite should comprise a compact unit, especially if only one teacher is responsible for supervising all of the activities.

Though convenient access to the rest of the school is a factor, a certain degree of isolation may be desired to avoid disturbing other classes or to allow use of the music unit at night when the rest of the building is locked. Separate music buildings provide some of these features, but they sacrifice ease of travel to the rest of the school. Fine arts centers in campus-type schools serve as solutions in some situations.[2]

In the preliminary discussions with the architect, the music staff should express preferences regarding the location of various elements in the music department as

2. See page 20 for a further discussion of combined facilities for the fine arts.

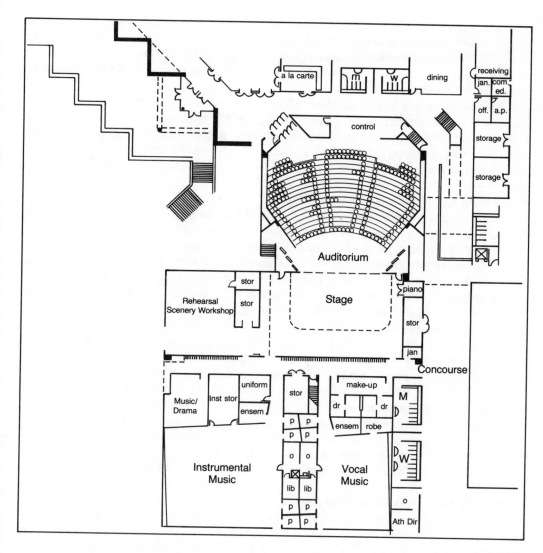

Auditorium

control

Stage

Rehearsal
Scenery Workshop

stor

stor

piano

stor

jan

Concourse

Music/
Drama

Inst stor

uniform

ensem

stor

make-up

dr   dr

ensem robe

M

Instrumental
Music

p p

p p

o o

lib lib

p p

p p

Vocal
Music

W

o

Ath Dir

a la carte

m   W

dining

receiving

jan. com.
ed.

off. a.p.

storage

storage

Creston High School, Grand Rapids, Michigan. Music facilities should be located near the auditorium with convenient access to the rest of the school. Architects: Daverman Associates. Acoustics: Geerdes Consulting Services.

well as the department's location in relation to the total school. They clearly should understand, however, that once the first lines are drawn on paper certain commitments for sound isolation and acoustics are already implied that may influence the excellence of the facility. The counsel of a competent acoustical consultant is invaluable, particularly at this early stage. One of the biggest problems in school planning is the fact that many states do not pay for consultants, and school boards often are not prepared to pay their fees. As a result, if the consultant is hired at all, often he or she is not retained until the project is too far along for him or her to be of maximum service. Some architects are reluctant to add another person whose input must be considered in each planning decision, and they prefer to execute the project alone. But the employment of experienced consultants as early as possible is an essential prerequisite to a successful music building. Additionally, these experts have much to offer in planning ordinary classrooms, offices, and other spaces in the modern school building.

Undesirable locations

A stage built in conjunction with a gymnasium and used as a music room is both acoustically and aesthetically undesirable. Scheduling problems are certain to arise from such a compromise: A music rehearsal cannot be conducted during gym classes or athletic practice. Curtains and room dividers *cannot* provide a sufficient sound barrier. Multipurpose rooms are not suitable for music use unless they first are designed as music rooms and have other activities carried on within them (not the reverse, which is more common). If at all possible, separate facilities should be provided for dissimilar activities.

Basement locations are undesirable because of possible dampness (that could damage valuable instruments), poor lighting, and often inconvenient access. Even more importantly, the low ceilings that typify a basement result in unsuitable acoustics, except for possible practice rooms. Also, noisy mechanical equipment is often located there, which is hard to isolate from spaces used for music.

BUILDING SECURITY AND PARKING

Some basic decisions related to traffic control and building security must be made early in the planning stage. Tight security in the music area can become a preponderant design consideration, and it should be studied very carefully. Many potential problems can be thwarted by careful forethought. Will there be times in the evening or on weekends when only the music facilities of the building will be used? Will rest rooms be available? What will be the schedule of keys for the building? It may be wise, for example, to place certain auxiliary areas (instrument storage, music library, or repair room) on the same key as the instrument rehearsal hall so that certain personnel can move freely with one key. By answering questions such as these, annoying inconveniences or lack of proper security can be avoided.

Careful planning also is needed with respect to parking. Although this area is not a concern of only the music department, there are certain aspects of the music program that may have special bearing on parking decisions. These aspects include whether the music organizations will perform away from school, and whether heavy equipment needs to be moved; whether the department will present evening programs in the recital hall or auditorium; whether community groups will use the music suite at night; and, whether noise in the parking area will disturb music study.

CONVERTING AND REMODELING

Schools sometimes are faced with the possibility of converting existing buildings, such as old auditoriums, gymnasiums, or cafeterias, into music facilities. It has been done successfully, but only in cases where a feasibility study by professionals has determined that the building is capable of being remodeled and what the right way is to do it (see chapter seven).

OUTDOOR CONCERT SITES

Schools and communities frequently plan for outdoor musical performance areas. One aspect of outdoor music performance that sometimes is overlooked is the need for a quiet site. It is hopeless to try to perform music outdoors in a noisy part of the city. In some instances the performance can be amplified to override the high level of traffic noise, but this too easily can become a caricature, not a real performance. Successful outdoor concert facilities are always in quiet locations, which are becoming increasingly hard to find.

COMBINED FACILITIES FOR THE FINE ARTS

Many schools are establishing fine arts departments that house art, drama, and music in units separate from the classroom area. Buildings of this nature usually consist of music, drama, and visual arts complexes. Dance may also be included. The intricacy of these buildings requires the selection of an architect with specialized knowledge of theater construction, an acoustical consultant, and a theater consultant to work with the architect from the initial planning through construction and completion. Only by this type of team planning can a project be assured of quality

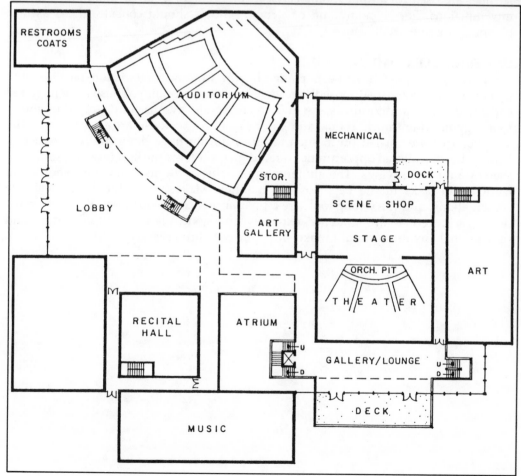

Above: Outdoor concerts continue to be an important factor in American life. Photograph by Wenger Corporation.
Left: Indiana College Fine Arts Center, Huntington. Combined facilities for the fine arts usually include areas for music, drama, and art. Architect: The InterDesign Group. Acoustics: Geerdes Consulting Services.

construction and satisfactory results. The drama complex may consist of a small theater with a capacity of 300 to 500, a workroom, dressing areas, one or more classrooms, storage rooms, laboratories, offices, museum and display areas, a library, storage, offices, and facilities for security personnel. The size and extent of these units depends on the student enrollment, community needs, and teacher orientation. In some areas of the country, fine arts departments are experiencing the most rapid growth in their history. In planning visual arts areas, one should not overlook photography laboratories, sculpture classrooms, shops for various crafts, and other forms of arts and crafts in the community.

Another aspect of the music/drama/art/dance complex is that of combined festivals that can extend over several weeks. These productions require highly specialized facilities that may result in a total community effort. Sufficient space is needed for musical extravaganzas such as symphonic drama, dance/drama, ballet, and historical revues. Since such events often make special demands on facilities, builders should thoroughly investigate the musical and dramatic background of those architectural, acoustical, and engineering consultants who are to advise on construction.

SPECIAL USES OF FINE ARTS FACILITIES

There has been an increasing emphasis on education from kindergarten through adulthood. People of all ages are attending college and secondary school. In fact, entire families are going to school, from the youngest in nursery schools to grandparents in graduate seminars. This changing picture of education demands a more efficient use of buildings and facilities. In college, recital halls and auditoriums are used by students a high percentage of the day. In public schools, these same facilities are used for adult evening classes, conferences, lectures, and other community functions. For economy and efficiency, schools should consider these uses in planning the fine arts facilities.

UNDESIRABLE COMBINATIONS

School in the past have been planned with various combination facilities that involved music rooms, supposedly in the interests of economy. These have included combinations of auditorium stage and music room, gymnasium/auditorium/music room, gymnasium/music room, and cafetorium. All of these are undesirable. The activities that are carried on in such facilities do not have the same requirements. Unless the educational opportunities offered give students the best learning situation, there are no real savings. The students must achieve the most for their efforts and learn to do tasks in the best possible manner. Makeshift buildings, undesirable combinations, and the wrong tools are a poor approach to education. Economy must not be achieved at the students' expense, and good planning by educators and professional architects should make such practices unnecessary.

INSTRUCTIONAL AREAS

Music facilities can be divided into three general categories: those used for instructional activities, those serving in an auxiliary capacity, and those used for public performances. A typical music facility for a large school requires a wide variety of rooms and work areas. The needs of smaller schools probably are somewhat less but incorporate many of the same functional areas by telescoping or combining them into compact layouts.

INSTRUMENTAL REHEARSAL ROOMS

An instrumental rehearsal room must be large enough to accommodate the biggest band, orchestra, or combined group expected to use the facility, plus a vacant space of no less than six feet around the periphery of the room. Marching bands place special space requirements on the room. Bands normally range from 80 to 120 players. It is not unusual, however, to find groups containing as many as 180 players. Orchestra space requirements are different, because string players require considerably more room. If community groups plan to use the facility, a larger rehearsal room with additional storages spaces may be needed.

Floor space is a requirement that needs much attention. Sound levels produced by an instrumental ensemble literally can be deafening. This is particularly true if amplified instruments are used. There are two ways of reducing these levels to a degree where effective rehearsing is possible: Provide adequate volume by ensuring ample floor area and ceiling height; and ensure that adequate sound-absorbant materials are appropriately distributed on wall and ceiling surfaces.

Room size

Floor area dimensions are determined by the number of students and whether they play wind or string instruments. An average figure of twenty-five to thirty square feet per student is desirable. Twenty square feet is the absolute minimum for winds and thirty square feet is minimal for orchestra. This footage provides the necessary space for aisles, piano, music stands, and other equipment. The square footage per player allowed for a smaller ensemble should be somewhat more than for a large group, because circulation space requirements do not decrease proportionately. Students should not sit against a wall or stand within seven and one-half feet of the ceiling. This is especially true of the bass horns and percussion instruments that often are placed on the highest riser in the back of the ensemble.

Ceiling height

Although the height of an instrumental rehearsal room depends on the number of students involved, the overall geometry of the room is also important. A frequent

Kalamazoo Christian High School, Kalamazoo, Michigan. This room is ideal for both choral and instrumental groups. There is an additional six feet above the suspended ceiling that is open around the four sides to the full ceiling height. The dropped ceiling is partially reflective and partially absorptive. The splayed front walls help disperse sound across the ensemble. Heavy adjustable acoustical draperies on two side walls and absorption above rear wall storage cabinets complete the acoustical elements in the design of this room. Consultant: Geerdes Consulting Services.

mistake in building rehearsal rooms is a lack of sufficient ceiling height. Ceiling height must be planned for acoustical purposes. The effect of built-in or portable risers on the ceiling height must not be overlooked. An average ceiling height of twenty-two to thirty feet is desirable. Heights of less than eighteen feet should be considered only if sufficient floor space is provided to yield a volume in excess of 400 cubic feet per student. Anything less than a fourteen-foot ceiling in an instrumental rehearsal room should be seriously questioned. Even an eighteen-foot ceiling seldom produces a volume requirement of 600 to 700 cubic feet per student, which studies have shown is necessary for loudness levels to remain within comfortable limits.

Ceiling reflective surfaces

Regardless of volume and sound-absorption considerations, some appropriate overhead surfaces must be provided that reflect sound from one musician to another in order to maintain balance and good ensemble acoustics. This is contrary to the general practice of placing acoustical tile on the entire ceiling area. Some ceiling reflection is essential to communication between players, especially if the volume of the room is large. If the ceiling height is over twenty to twenty-two feet, a partial ceiling should be suspended sixteen feet above the finished floor. The lighting fixtures, a mix of absorptive and reflective ceiling panels, and ventilating fixtures should be contained in this partial ceiling. There should be a space of six to eight feet left open all around the ceiling periphery, maintaining the full height. The outer four feet of this suspended ceiling should have a three and one-half inch blanket of dense sound-absorbing fiberglass laid above it to partially deaden the live space. The upper space is important because it accommodates the high sound/power level of a large band or orchestra. The lowered ceiling area helps students hear across the band or orchestra by providing important nearby reflections.

Risers

There are different opinions on the desirability of providing risers in instrumental

A high ceiling is essential to accommodate the high sound/power level of a large high school or college band.

rooms. If risers are desired, portable units are the wisest option, since permanent risers are inflexible and unchangeable, and do not permit optimal use of the room by a marching band. Permanent risers also limit all future users to the fixed configuration. Since rehearsal rooms generally survive a number of different directors, building permanent risers is not advisable. Regardless whether flat floors or permanent risers are used, the determination must be made early in the planning stage so that appropriate adjustments can be made in the other elements of the room design. If risers are built up from the grade level of the rest of the building, additional room height will be required. If the instrumental room is on the ground floor, additional ceiling height can be achieved by excavating out below grade.

Floors

The relative merits of carpet, wood, and tile for rehearsal room floors are continually being debated. The thin, easily maintained carpet usually found in school buildings has little acoustical value other than slightly reducing high-frequency sound while quieting chair movement and foot-scraping. Since performances seldom take place on carpeted floors, adjustments on the part of musicians and conductors who have become accustomed to rehearsing on carpet would have to be made. Many conductors believe the vibrational response of wood floors provides a tactile condition that aids group ensemble. The only advantages of tile floors are cost and maintainability, and many studies have challenged even these. If the room is to be used for orchestra rehearsals or cello classes, end-pin guards must be used to protect the tile or wood flooring. If end-pin guards are not available, pieces of foot-square rubber-backed carpeting can be used.

Acoustical considerations

Room acoustics are discussed in detail in chapter four, but a few preliminary comments are in order here as precautions. A rehearsal room, unlike an auditorium, is a teaching space in which such things as poor attacks, faulty intonation, and poor tone must be identified and corrected. A good rehearsal room should not duplicate the acoustics of a large performance hall. Room proportion and shape are critical and best left to the trained acoustician. Sound-absorbing materials should be located in areas other than just the ceiling and some of it should be located in the height zone at the sound source.

Ideally, bands and orchestras should not use the same rehearsal room. Research has indicated that for teaching purposes, the band requires a much less reverberant space than does an orchestra. Also, the sound/power level of a band can be considerably greater than that of an orchestra, and a larger room volume is required to keep the sound at a tolerable level. Few schools, however, can afford the luxury of separate band and orchestra rooms. If scheduling permits, one room can be made to serve both functions satisfactorily by minor space compromises and by the introduction of relatively inexpensive variable acoustical elements. Bands have a predominance of sound energy concentrated in the lower frequencies, especially in the low brass instruments, that makes it difficult to avoid "boominess" in most band rooms. Orchestras present less of a problem. Consequently, the room should be designed basically for band, with movable panels of appropriate materials to help liven the room for full orchestra and string rehearsals.

Taylor University, Upland, Indiana. The ceiling of this instrumental rehearsal room is twenty-two feet above the floor, with a dropped ceiling at sixteen feet with a mix of reflective and absorptive surfaces. The side and rear walls are treated with a shredded wood fiber absorptive material that is resistant to impact. Architects: The Troyer Group. Acoustics: Geerdes Consulting Services.

Other considerations

Heating and ventilating are discussed in detail in chapter four, but it should be mentioned here that year-round temperatures held at 68° to 74° and humidity held at 40 to 50 percent by a quiet air-handling system are essential in instrumental rooms— for the good of the instruments as well as for the comfort of the players. If the instrumental rehearsal room is to be used for theory or other music classes, mounted chalkboards may be advisable (acoustical considerations may require that their area be kept to a minimum or that they be covered by draperies or other adjustable absorption). Since rehearsal is the principal function of the room, no decision should be made that will detract from its ability to fulfill that role. For example, posture chairs with operable or detachable tablet arms should be purchased rather than chairs suitable for classroom use.

RECORDING AND PLAYBACK SYSTEMS

Provisions for tape recording and record, tape, and compact disc playback systems should be included in room plans so that the proper conduit can be installed at the time of construction. Provisions for closed-circuit television, movies, and slide projection also should be considered. Many rehearsal rooms currently incorporate

Calvin College, Grand Rapids, Michigan. Ceiling height can be increased in ground floor rehearsal rooms by excavating below grade. Architects: The Perkins and Will Partnership, Daverman Associates. Acoustics: Artec Consultants.

microphone outlets with conduit and proper wiring leading to a recording room. These use a talk-back system to provide two-way contact with the recording technician. Electrical requirements for audiovisual equipment are best met with separate circuits dedicated solely to powering it.

CHORAL REHEARSAL ROOMS

The specialized requirements of choral rehearsal rooms are different from those of facilities used exclusively for instrumental groups except in terms of temperature, humidity, and acceptable noise levels. Space requirements differ, because it is not necessary to provide floor area for music stands and instruments. Also, the sound/power level of instrumental groups is not equalled by vocal ensembles.

Room size

Each member of the choral group needs at least ten to twelve square feet of space if chairs are used on risers that are no less than thirty-two inches deep. If deeper risers are preferred (thirty-six or forty-inch), extra space must be planned, with fifteen to twenty square feet per person. Reference to manufacturer's catalogs of portable risers will give estimates of space requirements for risers of different dimensions and types of room layouts.

Ceiling height

Choral room ceilings do not have to be as high as those in instrumental rooms, but should be no less than fourteen to sixteen feet and preferably more. Sufficient volume and ceiling height should be planned to provide a brighter and more reverberant acoustical environment in the choral room than in the instrumental room. The effectiveness and flexibility of the room can be enhanced by moveable acoustical panels.

Risers

Large choral groups generally rehearse or perform using risers. Risers avoid obstructing the tone of singers in the back rows with the bodies of singers in front, and they also are essential for observing the conductor. An elevation of six to ten inches and a depth of forty inches is adequate for permanent or semipermanent choral risers. The architect should also be aware of the local building code and safety regulations in regard to risers. As in the instrumental room, portable risers offer greater flexibility than permanent ones.

Miscellaneous equipment

Since piano accompaniment often plays an important role in the choir rehearsal and performance, the room should provide space for a grand piano. Since some directors prefer to have their groups stand for at least part of the rehearsal, as well as for concerts, there should be enough flat floor space in front of the room to accommodate concert risers. Seats in the choral room should ensure proper low-back support for the singers, and folding tablet armchairs are useful for both classroom and rehearsal functions. Special fixed, theater-type seats with drop tablet arms allow a width of thirty-six inches between rows. Using the choral room for nonrehearsal functions suggests the inclusion of chalkboards, a projection screen, closed-circuit television, and videocassette recorder. Provisions also should be made for a tape/record/compact disc/cassette playback system with microphone outlets for recording and broadcasting.

VOCAL/INSTRUMENTAL ROOMS

Acoustically, one room cannot serve for both vocal and instrumental rehearsals with completely satisfactory results. Some communities, however, employ only one

teacher and cannot provide separate space for instrumental and vocal groups. In fact, in many one-teacher situations, one room is the nucleus of all music activities. In small music departments, a single, all-purpose room can be planned in terms of space to accommodate vocal and instrumental group rehearsals, small ensembles, individual rehearsals, a library, instrument and equipment storage, instrument repair facilities, an office, and a teaching studio, as well as other music classes. In terms of acoustics, however, these activities cannot be housed adequately in one room. Optimally, the room should be designed for band, because of the need to control the high sound level. Variable acoustical control will add little to the cost of the room, and adjustable acoustic draperies or wall panels will help the room serve acceptably for the choir and other needs. The room always will be a compromise, but it will be less so if this order of priorities is established. If such a combination room cannot be avoided, its eventual use as an instrumental music room should be kept in mind, with expansion to separate facilities as the ultimate goal.

A teaching studio requires more floor space than a practice room and additional creature comforts.

TEACHING STUDIOS

Although group instruction is an important facet of the music program, ideal choral and instrumental programs supplement their group work with private study by their more talented and serious students. Some provision for this must be made when designing the building. The sound isolation and acoustical requirements for a teaching studio are somewhat like those for a practice room. Because of frequent interruptions in singing or playing for conversation between teacher and student, and because of the more concentrated effort expended in the private lesson, the acoustical

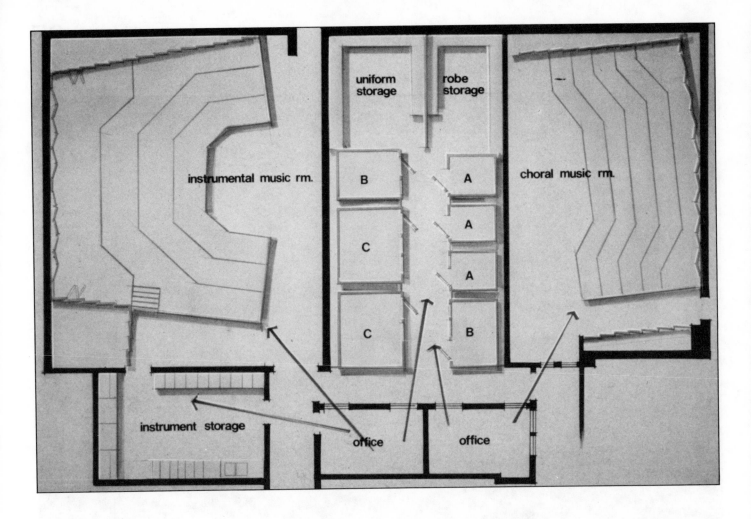

instrumental music rm.

uniform storage

robe storage

choral music rm.

B

A

A

C

A

C

B

instrument storage

office

office

Practice rooms should be placed together in a group near the rehearsal facilities. Photograph by Wenger Corporation.

criteria should be applied more stringently. For example, better sound isolation, more careful consideration of desirable acoustical ambience in multipurpose studios, and critical observance of noise criteria in the ventilation system are all needed in a good teaching studio.

A teaching studio requires more floor space than a practice room. An acceptable guideline for an average studio is 200 to 250 square feet. Some consideration should be given to the sound-power levels of different performance media, for a pipe organ studio or percussion studio will have different requirements than a voice or piano studio. Customizing teaching studios to suit individual teachers is possible through the use of portable sound-absorbing panels that are hung from a wall rail. These can be included in the building design, or they can be constructed inexpensively in a school shop.

PRACTICE ROOMS

Practice rooms are spaces peculiar to music, and their design demands special consideration not necessary in other rooms. Among these are number, location, size and shape, ventilation, and provisions for supervision.

Number

The number of practice rooms needed by a music department should be related to the number of students involved and the school policy regarding practice room use. Some authorities recommend that students practice in school as much as possible where assistance and supervision are available. Many feel that it is particularly important for students who play large instruments to have practice facilities available because of the difficulty in carrying these instruments home. The number of practice rooms needed may be determined by a survey and an estimate of needed hours per school day. As a rule of thumb, a minimum of one practice room should be provided for every forty students enrolled in the school's performance groups; a maximum of one room for each twenty students should be provided in an active program that stresses individual practice at school.

Location

Practice rooms should be convenient to the large rehearsal room to minimize moving heavy instruments and to maximize supervision. Efficient use of the rooms is possible, however, only if they are located and constructed so that good isolation of their sound is achieved. Placing practice rooms along one wall of the rehearsal room is a highly questionable practice, since neither the doors nor the glass needed for supervision can provide the required level of sound control, and the simultaneous use of both areas is less than satisfactory. Practice rooms should be placed by themselves in a group, with a library or storage rooms between them and the rehearsal hall. The least-expensive and best way to achieve good sound isolation is the provision of a buffer zone between the spaces where incompatible activities are to be carried on. Special construction techniques are required in the walls, floors, ceilings, doors, and heating and ventilating systems. During construction, particular care must be taken to ensure that the rooms are airtight, which makes them soundtight. Masonry construction is advisable, with furred gypsum board or plaster skins applied to increase isolation. Applying gypsum board to plaster systems that do not employ masonry should not be used. This is true for rooms to be used for vocal as well as instrumental practice, because the piano, with its percussive attack and wide frequency range, is one of the most difficult instruments to isolate. With the increasing use of amplified instruments in schools, proper location, careful design, and meticulous construction of practice rooms is more critical than ever.

Size and shape

Practice rooms vary in size according to their function. Individual practice rooms of fifty-five to sixty-five square feet are quite satisfactory, although that size does not consider the extra space beyond that needed for an upright piano, a chair, and a music stand. With the need for ensemble and sectional rehearsals, several larger practice rooms of 300 to 350 square feet that can be shared by vocal and instrumental groups should be included. These rooms could accommodate a grand piano or a small pipe organ. Parallel walls must be avoided in practice rooms unless corrected by considerable sound-absorbing treatment that is effective at low, middle, and high frequencies. The important effect of size, shape, and wall and ceiling treatments on the acoustics of practice rooms is discussed in detail in chapter four.

VENTILATION

Air-conditioning is becoming standard in schools throughout the country. This is not only an improvement to the ventilation system in what often are cramped quarters, but it also provides an incidental boost to the effectiveness of sound isolation between rooms. Practice rooms can be arranged in compactly spaced blocks, and even planned without outside windows. Temperature and humidity should be controlled in practice rooms at the same levels as in classrooms with closed windows. Special attention must be paid to the duct layout and treatment of the air-handling system to prevent excessive fan noise and transfer of sound between rooms. The gentle sound of moving air can mask intruding sounds from neighboring rooms and is a useful tool if carefully implemented. In fact, some music buildings are including electronic noise generators for this very purpose, with a volume control so that the aspiring cellist can cover up the sound of the adjacent soprano with a pleasant purr. Practice rooms will cost more to construct than ordinary classrooms because of the extra cost of measures required to ensure adequate sound isolation, but monetary cutbacks are less justifiable here than in any other part of the music suite.

PREFABRICATED PRACTICE ROOMS

Ready-made practice rooms are the answer of today's technology to the many difficulties encountered in building good practice rooms on-site. They are variably sized, have adequate in-room acoustics, and are guaranteed by the manufacturer (who is also the installer) to provide excellent sound isolation between rooms. They are often used in remodeling projects in which an existing open rooms is converted into small practice rooms. A small gymnasium, for example, can be converted into a bilevel practice suite through their use. Providing sound isolation, acoustical treatment, lighting, and ventilation, these units depend only on the air-handling equipment of the space in which they stand and access to an electrical outlet. In either new or remodeling projects, they can provide a flexibility that permanent construction cannot achieve, while giving the appearance of regular built-in rooms. Size, shape, and height are all variable. Even more important, all critical isolation and acoustic criteria are met with guaranteed results. If construction costs are high, it may be less expensive to buy and install these portable units than to use conventional construction methods. The consistency of their acoustical results is hard to match.

MUSIC CLASSROOMS

Regular academic classrooms are often used for classes in music history, appreciation, theory, composition, arranging, or other nonperformance subjects. If the teaching of these classes involves listening to music, these rooms are seldom completely satisfactory. For these uses, greater than ordinary care must be taken to block out extraneous sounds and to keep the noise level of the ventilating system below that normally allowed. The acoustics of the room also should provide for easy and pleasant listening, so a certain amount of liveness is desirable; acoustic tile should not be applied indiscriminately over the entire ceiling area.

Left: Prefabricated practice rooms can be especially useful in remodeling projects. Photograph by Wenger Corporation.

Right: Music classroom ceilings should be treated with acoustic tile only around the outer area with the center hard and reflective for better singing and listening conditions.

A classroom used primarily for general music classes needs ample storage space for books, records, rhythm instruments, Autoharps, piano keyboards, pictures, and similar equipment. Each such room should have a projection screen in a recessed ceiling pocket with electric outlets in convenient places for easy use of projection equipment. If a classroom is to be used for theory classes, it is helpful to have staff lines painted on most of the chalkboards. However, this should not be done if music literature or appreciation classes will be the principal users of the room. Classrooms for college music education will need adequate locked shelf space or an adjacent

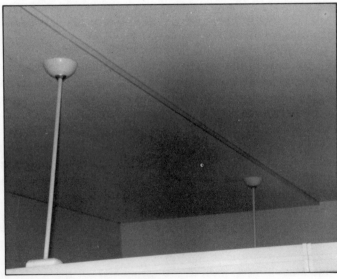

storage room with shelves to accommodate large amounts of material. Campus-type schools and colleges also should consider supplying coat hooks, lockers, and shelf space in each classroom.

OPEN SCHOOLS

Most music teachers are accustomed to having their own rooms and teaching within those four walls. Such conditions are not found in some open schools. The flexibility of few fixed walls and the effect of such design on the activities carried on within them are educational developments of the twentieth century. Conventional approaches to the use of unconventional spaces do not always work. It is not within the scope of this book to discuss the philosophy or accomplishments of the open school. It can be helpful, however, to make a few general observations.

Any activity that involves formal lecture teaching can be acceptable in the open room. As long as similar activities are going on in adjacent spaces, problems will be minimized as long as adequate distance exists. Such activities as playing instruments or listening to recordings over a conventional sound system are not possible, since a high enough volume level for satisfactory listening would be above the general sound

Wagram Primary School, Scotland County, North Carolina. The "Theatrette" is an innovative concept for elementary schools, seating 150 students, with directional lighting, built-in risers, and acoustical treatment that makes it a very functional space. Architect: Boney Architects. Photograph by Fred Wilkins.

Multiple electronic keyboard units can be stored easily at the back of a regular music classroom.

level of other activities in the large space. A zoned system, with many loudspeakers playing at low level, will work reasonably well only if very generous spaces exist between activities. Ideally, each student should be provided with a high-fidelity headset. An equipment unit housing tape-, record-, cassette-, or compact disc-playing facilities may feed into headphone outlets in the pupil area for young children or to tabletops or carrels for older students. This system can offer a number of advantages, since it makes individualized instruction and the use of self-teaching materials possible.[3]

Aside from these talking or listening activities, most music teaching requires performance, and this *must* be accommodated by special music rooms with the traditional four walls to confine the sound and to provide proper acoustics for effective rehearsal. Some educational facility planners may feel that music teachers are not being progressive by insisting on such spaces, but imagining the effects of a band rehearsal on all other teaching in an open space should settle the argument quickly.

CLASS PIANO ROOMS

Many school systems provide class instruction in piano as well as in band and orchestra instruments. The increasing availability of electronic keyboard instruments has made this practical even in smaller schools. A special room for this activity should be provided to accommodate either acoustic or electronic pianos. A room for group instruction or regular pianos imposes many requirements in terms of sound isolation because the percussive action of the piano and the full range of its sound (both in frequency and in dynamics) make it one of the most difficult instruments to contain.

3. This material is revised from the author's chapter, "The Environment for Learning," in *Individualized Instruction in Music*, compiled by Eunice Boardman Meske and Carroll Reinhart (Washington, D.C.: Music Educators National Conference, 1975).

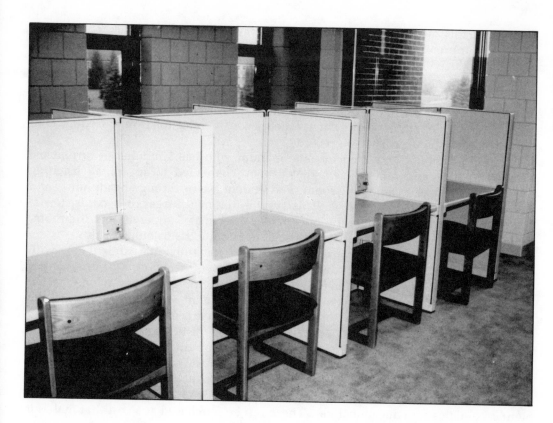

Listening stations can be operated from a central position using headphones picked up from the operator and plugged into an individual volume control. A work space for scores and notebooks is a convenient feature.

Multiplying the number of pianos increases this problem. Careful consideration must be given to sound conditioning, with acoustical treatment of the walls and ceilings and special insulation against transmitting sound to and from adjacent music classrooms. The room also will require chalkboards (both plain and with music staves), bulletin boards, music cabinets, and sufficient electrical outlets. Recording and playback facilities for television, records, cassettes, tapes, and compact discs also should be provided.

Electronic keyboards are becoming more popular because they offer many advantages over conventional pianos. In spite of their limited range, different touch, and the electronic quality of their sound, electronic keyboards have been improved in quality since their inception. A survey of models on the market will indicate instruments with expanded range, more typical piano touch, and acceptable sound. One great advantage is their lower cost, the possibility of using portable multiple-keyboard units, teacher/pupil contact via headsets, the possibility of playing records and tapes over the system, and the fact that almost any room can be used.

The ideal room for such use possesses certain amenities, such as carpeting and some sound-absorbent wall treatments. Careful planning of the room layout will enhance its efficient use. Choose the manufacturer and model in advance, because keyboard dimensions vary. In-floor and in-wall cable runs will make it possible to avoid treacherous, unsightly wires on the floor. Equipment manufacturers can help with details of advance planning, and teachers and administrators should not hesitate to take advantage of their services.

LISTENING FACILITIES

As independent study becomes more common in open elementary and high school classrooms, providing a listening center at these levels becomes much more important than when this facility typically was found only at the college level. There are a number of approaches to the design and use of a listening center, and they are not mutually exclusive. Three of these approaches follow:

- A number of soundproofed listening rooms or cubicles are provided, each with a tape, cassette, or record player. The student signs out material from a central location, such as the music department office or the resource center in the library, and is his own operator. This system exacts a considerable toll from the equipment and recordings, particularly on records.
- A central position is provided for one operator who has a number of turntables, cassette decks, and tape players that can be channeled to any or all listening positions in this or an adjoining room. The student listens through headphones and does not handle source material. This system minimizes wear on records, tapes, and equipment, and permits the operator to double as a supervisor in the room. However, it does require special personnel to operate the listening facility.
- A bank of tape players or cassettes is installed for individual student use with earphones, while the majority of listening stations are fed from a central control position. In this way, assignments that require stopping and replaying selected portions of a tape may be completed by the student without recourse to the operator. These stations serve the autotutorial approach particularly well.

Designing a listening center is becoming a highly sophisticated and challenging job because of rapid changes in the field of storing and reproducing music. Two-channel stereophonic equipment of the highest fidelity is a must. Although cassette players once were adequate only for recording speech, today's high-quality tapes, improved equipment, and low-noise and noise-reducing electronics are excellent and convenient capabilities for educational use. These can be purchased at a cost that makes it possible for students to borrow from the school or have their own private cassette listening center. The savings in room, personnel, and electronics might better be met by having a cassette duplicator, provided its use does not violate copyright law. Whatever equipment is installed, it should be open-ended and designed for the most flexibility so that new technical developments can be incorporated as they occur. Obsolescence is probably a greater threat here than in any other area of the music facility.

The equipment to be used, the number and kind of listening stations, and the desired atmosphere in the room all will have a bearing on its layout. To avoid the institutional look, use tables, lamps, and comfortable furniture to give the appearance of lounges or living rooms. Attention should be given in advance to the special electrical needs for such a room. Ideally, the room should be quite dead acoustically because most if not all listening will be done with headphones.

ELECTRONIC MUSIC STUDIOS

Will the new facility provide space and equipment for the composition of electronic music? Most large universities and many small ones today have studios staffed by faculty members qualified to work and teach in this booming field. A more specific discussion of equipment needs for the electronic music studio is found in chapter eight. The room should be acoustically dead because of high monitoring levels and the need to avoid coloration of the sound by room effects. It also should be very well insulated from other music rooms.

AUXILIARY AREAS

Offices

For a music program to function smoothly, there must be a conveniently located office. Frequently, it is placed adjacent to the rehearsal hall, with windows that enable the director to view either rehearsals or practices. This location places severe but not impossible requirements on the shared wall and the window between the two areas. If the need for a quiet office is paramount, it should be either built with a sound lock (a vestibule at the entrance with acoustical doors at each end) or located off an adjacent work area that could serve the same purpose. The office should not contain music library files, repair facilities, or other equipment that will generate a great deal of student traffic. If the office is to double as a teaching studio, it must be large enough to accommodate a piano, several chairs, and a tape or cassette recorder, as well as filing cabinets, and perhaps other cabinets. In some situations, the office may be called upon to double as a recording control room. In this case, the necessary conduit for audio cables should be concealed in the floor or wall, and there should be extra electrical outlets. Ideally, there will be a separate room for recording, perhaps adjacent to the auditorium, but serving the rehearsal room as well.

Music teachers who teach in several locations in a school (for example, harmony in a classroom, choir in the recital hall, general music in a specially equipped center), also need an office to organize their many materials, instruments, and pieces of equipment. Offices are essential for department heads or for directors of performing groups because of the frequent contact they have with members of the community. The central offices of a college department or school of music reflect the organization and function of that particular department. If the offices provide only for administrative and secretarial staff, one size is indicated. If, in addition, the office area houses advisors, student records, and the like, a more complex unit is required. The service area for the central office may range from one supply closet to a well-equipped room with several types of duplicating and photocopying machines. It may include a checkout space for recordings and be adjacent to listening rooms; it also may provide a repository for the department's audiovisual equipment. If student inquiries are anticipated in large number, a counter may be planned in the office. This has the advantage of controlling office traffic, separating the office personnel from the public, and providing space under the counter for storage.

Storage areas

Adequate storage areas planned with traffic patterns in mind are important to the smooth functioning of a music facility. Storage with proper heat and humidity control is necessary for musical instruments, robes and uniforms, music scores, records, and various types of equipment. With careful planning, the storage areas can be placed conveniently and at the same time serve as buffers between two sound-producing areas, such as the instrumental and choral rehearsal halls.

Instrument storage

Instrument storage facilities should be located so as to minimize the moving of instruments. Careful attention should be given to traffic patterns of movement in the room, with sufficient free floor space and ample distribution of compartments to avoid bottlenecks. Storage cabinets located in rehearsal areas are inaccessible during rehearsal periods and frequently cause congestion during period changes. In some cases, this still might be the most advantageous location, in which case an extra 200 to 300 square feet of floor space should be allowed for them.

An instrument storage room should be at least twenty feet wide and thirty feet long. If there are windows, they should be placed high along one side. Glass block construction frequently is employed here. This type of window placement will permit the installation of cabinets of various depths placed along two or three of the walls below the windows. The size of the cabinets should not be more than a maximum of forty-eight inches deep, sixty-two inches wide, and eighty-three inches high. In some instances, it might be advantageous to extend cabinets to the ceiling or to have a second set of cabinets built over the lower group for storage of equipment that is used occasionally. A stepladder or rolling ladder should be kept on hand for reaching the high shelves. Storage units can be built in by the building contractor or purchased separately. If prebuilt units are used, care must be taken to ensure that the large units can pass through the door openings.

The instrument storage room should be well ventilated with a constant year-round temperature of 65° to 70°, and a relative humidity of 35 to 50 percent, which is optimal for wooden musical instruments with glued joints. While it is possible to provide only shelves for storing instruments, this practice is undesirable. Most instruments have removable parts that are easily broken or jarred loose, and these may be lost or stolen if instruments are not kept in compartments. The instrument storage room should connect directly with the instrumental music room.

Storage lockers made of wood or metal can be built to specifications for instruments and are available from manufacturers of storage equipment. If metal is used, carpeting should be affixed to the bottom of the cabinets to reduce noise and the possibility of damage, especially to large uncased brass instruments. Ventilation space should be provided in each locker door, and the compartments should be large enough to avoid hitting door edges when removing instruments. Folding doors built to extend over several cabinet fronts is another method of protecting instruments. Lockers should be constructed to promote ready access as well as to protect the instruments. Deep lockers can be built into the wall area of surrounding corridors. The shelves and compartments may be designed to suit the instrument and equipment needs, or attractive and sturdy commercial cabinets can be purchased. In either case, a depth of four feet and a height of six feet is adequate. Since most of the smaller musical instruments can be kept in regular student lockers, it may not be necessary to provide compartments for them. When these smaller instruments are not assigned to the students (such as during the summer), several instruments can be stored together in the large compartments.

Uniform and robe storage

Storage facilities are needed for school-owned band and orchestra uniforms, choir robes, or vestments. This closet space should be cedar-lined, and a well-constructed, close-fitting door will help protect against moths and dust. The closet space should be high enough so uniforms and robes will not touch the floor when hanging on racks, and some provision should be made to space them at equal intervals and to facilitate identification. A separate compartment for caps, belts, and other miscellaneous equipment also should be provided. If the director requires the band and choral uniforms to be left at school, dressing facilities should be located near the uniform storage area. For greater convenience, a set of portable folding racks can be set up, loaded with uniforms, and rolled down the hall from the storage room to the dressing rooms. The dressing rooms should be provided with bathing facilities, mirrors, and adequate dressing space. In some schools, these are rather elaborate facilities; in others, only minimum space is provided in the rest rooms. One possibility is to provide a workroom equipped with sewing machines and personnel to alter and repair uniforms. Such a room also may be used as a workshop for making minor instrument repairs. To facilitate equipment distribution, a shelf can be installed on the lower half of a Dutch door for the instrument and uniform storage rooms.

Music library

Music libraries range from a single set of filing cabinets in the music room to a library complete with stacks, reading rooms, charging desk, listening facilities, and work areas. In most colleges, there also are smaller libraries (band, orchestra, choral) that are more like the secondary school situations described here. Steel filing cabinets (full suspension with thumb locks) frequently are used for storing vocal and instrumental music. The letter-size file is satisfactory for choral music, whereas the legal-size file is desirable for most band and orchestra scores. Many schools use specially constructed cardboard boxes for music, allowing more wall space for storage. Box storage makes it possible to file new pieces in their proper places without shifting whole drawers of music to make space for the new purchases. Units that store the music flat also are available. Ensemble libraries tend to outgrow available space. A great space-saver consists of stacks that move on steel tracks, so only a single aisle is required to serve any number of storage units.

A sorting rack with five or six slanted shelves is valuable for distributing and arranging music for individual music folders; it also can serve as a folder cabinet. Music directors may prefer a specially constructed music folder cabinet that has individual compartments for each folio. This cabinet keeps the music orderly, facilitates music distribution and collection, makes possible a quick check of what music has been removed for individual practice, and provides a convenient means of carrying music from the rehearsal area to concert stage. The partitions should have semicircular recesses so that folders can be grasped easily. Some directors prefer folio cabinets with larger, vertical slots, each of which will hold the three to six folders needed for each section. In this way, only one-fifth to one-third of the players need to stop at the folio cabinet, and traffic flows more smoothly into and out of the room. The music library room should be separated from the instrument storage room. However, it usually is desirable and practical to have the two rooms adjoining, both opening off the music room, the stage, or both. Space in the library must be provided for work tables, supply cabinets, chairs, and a desk. In many smaller facilities, the music library equipment is kept in the office of the music director.

Instrument repair rooms

Some sort of facility should be provided for emergency instrument repairs. A special room is preferable, although a section of the music library or storage room or director's office may be used for this purpose. Larger school systems often have specially trained employees to take care of all instrument and equipment repairs. The

Ensemble libraries tend to outgrow available space. A great space saver consists of stacks that move on steel tracks, so only a single aisle is required to access any number of storage units.

College and university music departments should include a student lounge.

minimum provision should be a workbench with running water, a stool, and a supply of appropriate tools.

Duplicating rooms

Music departments usually have the facilities of the general office at their disposal, and there may not be the need for copying or duplicating equipment in the music suite itself. Most collegiate departments or schools of music and some school departments housed separately in a campus-type school find a duplicating room essential. There are many times when the music department needs items copied—rehearsal schedules, instrumental parts of a student composition, football show routines, trip itineraries, vocalises for the choir, songs in the public domain—and equipment should be readily available. The room should include enough counter space for several types of machines, an area for collating, and a sink.

ADDITIONAL FACILITIES

Because the music suite frequently is used at night when the remainder of the building is locked, some rest room facilities and custodial work areas must be provided within the music unit. In many instances, they are used as dressing rooms and must be convenient to the rest of the department. These facilities require about 15 percent of the total floor space if adequate room is to be provided. If public recitals are to be presented in the music unit, additional rest room space may be needed.

Collegiate music departments should consider the desirability of a lounge in which students can relax. If other study areas on the campus are some distance from the music facilities, one portion of the lounge might provide desk or table space.

Because of the heavy instruments and equipment that frequently must be moved in a music department, an elevator is desirable in a building of two or more floors. Also recommended is a loading dock adjacent to the parking area and as close to the auditorium stage as possible.

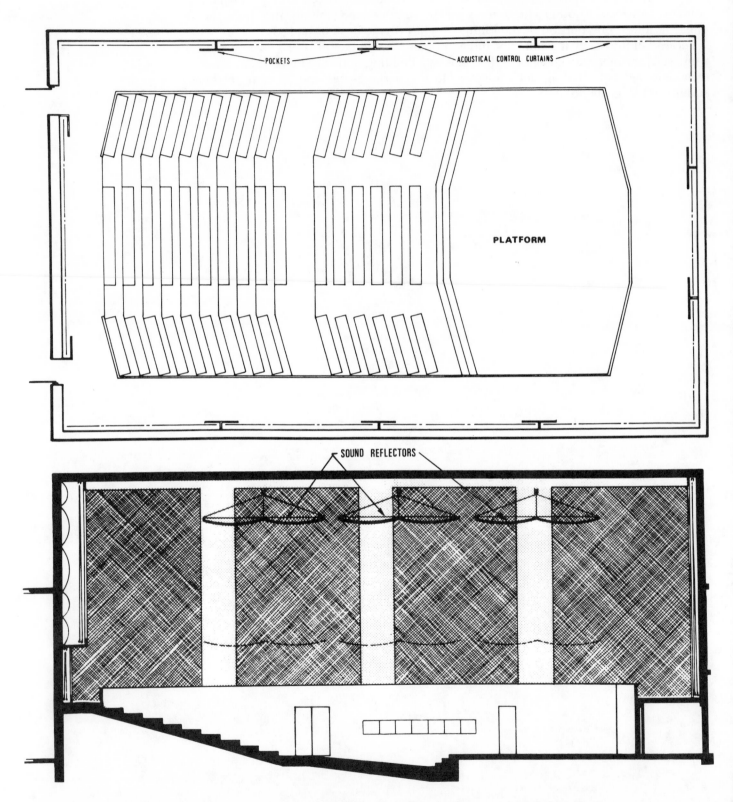

Floor plan and cross-section of a recital hall for music. Drawing courtesy of Artec Consultants.

CHAPTER 3

PERFORMANCE AREAS

RECITAL HALL

Any room intended for solo recitals, chamber music groups, or small ensembles may be termed a recital hall. Anything larger falls into the category of a theater or auditorium. Planning the recital hall begins with a decision about the hall's intended use and its seating capacity. These decisions will influence the size of the stage and bring about certain limitations of use. A hall seating only 250 people cannot have a stage large enough to accommodate an orchestra and chorus or even a large band. Such a small room would be uncomfortably loud with such powerful groups, even if space were available.

As with other large special-use rooms, one must think of a recital hall as also including several adjacent areas. Chief among these are performers' dressing rooms, provisions for pipe organ case work (if the hall will have an organ), a recording or broadcasting control room, storage rooms, warm-up areas, and a box office. In each case, the location of these and other special areas should be considered in relation to ease of concert operation. For example, a control room should have a view of the entire stage, and performers' rooms should be located on the same floor as the stage rather than a floor above or below; otherwise, both lose much of their convenience.

Once the seating capacity of the recital hall has been determined, its shape, proportions, and the like become concerns for the architect and the acoustical consultant. There are a number of practical suggestions. A lighting dimmer control panel should be provided offstage to dim audience lights during concerts. Separate circuits with wall switches that provide at least thirty footcandles of light should be available for classroom use of the hall. A telephone system should connect the backstage area with the box office for efficiency in concert operation. Doors leading from corridors into the wings and from the wings onto the stage must be wide enough to provide for the passage of a grand piano (a small detail, yet one that often has been missed). If the delivery of pianos or other large equipment is anticipated, the stage should have access to a loading dock. Even if the music building caters primarily to school audiences, proximity to parking areas should be considered.

Many recital halls double as classrooms or large lecture halls. Therefore, it may be necessary to provide theater-type seats with folding tablet arms so they can accommodate concert audiences and students. A large ceiling-mounted projection screen can be useful, as well as connections to a recording studio. Video, slide, and movie projectors should be located in a projection booth if at all possible.

REHEARSAL/RECITAL FACILITIES

As a room for music performance, the recital hall should be designed with strict criteria for sound isolation, adequate volume, sound treatment for proper acoustics, and a low level of ventilation noise. If it is well designed, it will include many of the requirements for an excellent rehearsal room. Combining recital and instrumental rooms is not as satisfactory as combining recital and choral rooms. The requirements of a good choral room and a good small recital hall are so compatible that they easily can be combined. The shallow stepped rows needed for a seated choir lend themselves well to audience seating without a lot of wasted space. This would not be true if the rows of seats were four feet apart as in a band or orchestra room. Fixed seating and a stage is essential for recitals, and a second lighting system that is dimmer-controlled will enhance the atmosphere and visual comfort. The stage easily can be made accessible for a choir on standing risers so they can rehearse in concert formation. Three or four steps across the front of the entire stage down to the audience seating level can serve as permanent standing risers.

The acoustics of a recital hall should be on the live side, which will favor choral singing. Recital halls need abundant volume to have excellent acoustics. Adjustable acoustical draperies should be used on at least two walls (not opposite each other) to make the room suitable for varying types of performances.

AUDITORIUM

Basic design considerations

The most important school performance area is the large concert room or auditorium. Of all the disappointments that can accompany the move into new facilities, none is more saddening than an inadequate auditorium, for it is there the music program meets the public, and all the intense effort and hard work should pay off. It is not easy to completely meet the objectives that seem so obvious to the staff during the planning stage. A tremendous amount of money is wasted when this fails to happen. Even more appalling is the fact that in future years, the students and the community will be deprived of the joy and inspiration that comes from performing in a fine hall; audiences will not receive the full benefits of performances; and the entire music program will be at a disadvantage. The planners, therefore, must approach the auditorium project with great care. Proper design will avoid creating facilities that are not suited to your particular needs, or that are designed for situations not appropriate for your communities. The auditorium should be designed for educational use, not for noneducational or commercial purposes.

Architects with experience in designing general facilities are not necessarily prepared to solve the problems associated with auditorium design. Those with experience in planning a movie theater or a community multipurpose hall also may not be qualified. The wise and prudent planner will use every resource available to ensure the success of the project. The planner should secure specialists in acoustics, theater planning, ventilation, and related fields to supplement the architectural staff. They are essential to the success of any project as complicated as an auditorium. Educational auditoriums must serve many functions usually carried out by amateurs. Design here is a particular challenge, since the special demands of amateurs often surpass those made by professionals.

Not to be overlooked is the necessity of providing access and seating for handicapped persons. An open space behind the back row and close to doors and rest rooms often makes good sense because it can easily be filled with movable seating for other patrons if needed. Two spaces per hundred seats should be allowed for handicapped seating. Additional considerations involved in accommodating persons with various handicaps are discussed in chapter three.

AUDIENCE-TO-STAGE RELATIONSHIP

There are four basic auditorium and theater designs, each of which puts the performers and observers in a different relationship. A discussion of these four types and their implications for musical performance follows.

Arena

The earliest theater form was the arena, sometimes called central stage or theater-in-the-round. This form places the audience around the stage on all sides. It is not suitable for school music performance, although there are a few concert halls of this type, such as the postwar Berlin Philharmonic Hall in Germany and the Boettcher Concert Hall in Denver. Poor instrumental balance for listeners seated behind the band or orchestra, generally poor onstage communication between players, and the loss of eye contact with many of the listeners are just three of the problems with this design.

Thrust stage

The three-quarter-round thrust stage does not provide a hospitable environment for most music performances. With the audience surrounding the stage on three sides, many of the objections to the arena apply here, including the impossibility of placing sound reflectors around the performers. A thrust stage also is unsatisfactory for music because of its dimensions. When properly designed for drama productions, it is no more than twenty feet wide and twenty-five feet deep, which will hardly accommodate the average band or orchestra. It may be suitable for chamber music and solo recitals, but it creates problems for young and untrained speaking voices and therefore is not an ideal form for school dramatists.

Proscenium stage

The proscenium stage, sometimes called the ''picture frame,'' has been a popular playhouse and concert hall form for several centuries. In it, the performers actually are in one room, and the audience is in another on the other side of the frame. The

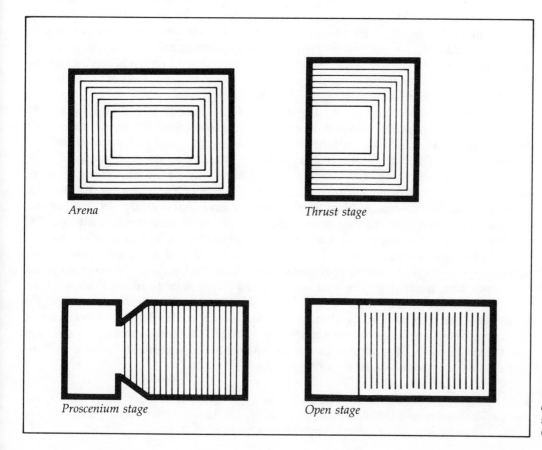

Arena

Thrust stage

Proscenium stage

Open stage

The four basic theater designs. Each puts the performers and audience in a different relationship. Drawing courtesy of Artec Consultants.

Macomb Community College Center for the Performing Arts, Mt. Clemens, Michigan. The proscenium stage places the performers in another room from the audience. Architects: TMP Associates. Acoustics: R. Lawrence Kirkegaard and Associates. Photograph by Balthazar Korab.

past eighty-five years of educational auditorium use in the United States have revealed many undesirable aspects of the large proscenium stage, particularly for music but also for many other common auditorium uses. A true proscenium must have a wide, tall stage house to be effective. This is necessary for acoustic coupling with the audience chamber, as well as for providing room for staging large-group performances and accommodating a stage rigging system. Not only is this large volume expensive, but it also places student musicians and actors out of scale where they are acoustically lost behind an arch that is fifty to sixty feet wide. Reducing the size of the arch visually with drapes or shutters is difficult and expensive, and it produces sightline problems unless the shape of the seating area also is changed. The typical proscenium is draped with heavy curtains and topped with a high stage house hung with sound-absorbing elements. Such a dead environment is hostile to music-making and demands a costly acoustical shell.

It is especially difficult to justify the wide arch, high stage house, and acoustical shell at a time when student-scaled, nonmechanized, multiform laboratory theaters of seventy-five to 150 seats are gaining favor among high school and college students and teachers.[4] Educational theater groups rarely produce all their plays in a 900- to 1,500-seat auditorium as they often were required to do in the past. If music ensembles must perform in a proscenium hall, some of the visual and acoustical problems can be avoided by placing instrumental and choral groups in front of the arch on large lifts. These can serve as a stage for drama or as audience seating areas and an orchestral pit when lowered to the appropriate levels. In this scheme, theater sets can be put behind a movable sound-isolating wall and remain in place while concert rehearsals and performances take place. Unfortunately, using several motorized stage lifts, movable walls, and seat wagons requires more funds than a school usually has to spend. However, it is far less costly than building two auditoriums. If it is not important to have daily changeover between concert and play rehearsals or performances, a forestage made of manually operated platforms can be designed for music performance. This may require removing several rows of seats (individually or in sections) and could not be done frequently.

---

4. This subject is covered extensively in Horace Robinson, *Architecture for the Educational Theatre* (Eugene: University of Oregon Press, 1971); and Richard Courtney, *The Drama Studio* (London: Pitman & Sons, 1963).

Open stage

With an open stage, the audience and performers are in one room, with the stage at one end. It is the most successful design for dual use by music and theater groups, and it is desirable for educational institutions where the auditorium must serve many different purposes. Most Western music was designed for similar rooms, and many of the world's finest concert halls use this format. Its advantages are many, including the considerable savings that result from the elimination of the costly stage house and shell. More funds can be invested in the stage and its equipment, and a great deal of flexibility can be built in. The overall shape of the walls, ceiling, and floor easily can be designed so that a heavy stage shell for band or orchestra is not needed. Opera and musical theater also can be set suitably in an open stage auditorium. The hard surfaces surrounding the stage help musicians hear each other and also reinforce speech. If space for shifting scenery is provided to the left and right of the stage, little or no flying equipment or fly space is required. Castered portable sound reflectors, and in some cases fixed or pivoting panels, will make the stage completely flexible for use by large or small musical groups or for play production. Acoustical adjustment through the use of heavy curtains or banners on the side and rear walls help adapt the room for certain music and speech performances requiring lower reverberation times (see chapter four).

Scenic projection, both lens and direct beam, becomes important in the open stage. This can be either front or rear projection, but provision must be made early in the design for the method of choice. The rear wall (upstage) must be considered both for its visual function and as a stage reflector. A piece of fabric can be hung over this as an occasional backdrop. Anything is acceptable, so long as the exposed surface provides a suitable background for concerts as well as theater. Catwalks provide access to lights and serve for temporary hanging of scenery. Curtain tracks provide for lateral movement of soft scenery. Pivoting sound-reflective panels stage right and left work for both music and speech.

The playing size of the stage should be determined by the size of the musical organizations, the stage requirements of musical or dramatic productions, and the

Calvin College Fine Arts Center, Grand Rapids, Michigan. With scene projection and an orchestra pit the open stage functions for drama as well as music. The open stage places the audience and the performers in the same room and eliminates the need for an expensive stage shell. Architects: The Perkins and Will Partnership, Daverman Associates. Acoustics: Artec Consultants.

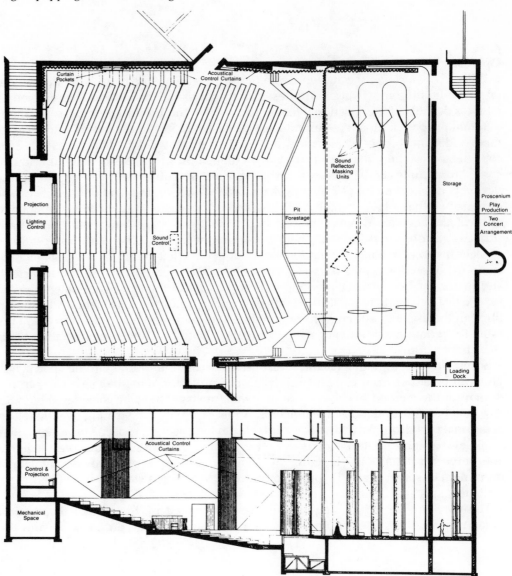

Floor plan and cross-section of an open stage auditorium. Drawing courtesy of Artec Consultants.

scope of other proposed activities. An orchestral musician should be allotted eighteen square feet of floor space for himself, his instrument, and his music stand. This is a generally accepted figure for the minimum seating area, and it is much less than that recommended for the rehearsal hall because extra space at the front of the room is not needed here. A 100-piece orchestra requires about 1,800 square feet of floor space, or an area about fifty feet wide and thirty-six feet deep. The space requirements for band are about the same. The stage will have to be proportionately large to accommodate combined choral and orchestral groups. The music educators must supply the architect with this kind of information.

SINGLE OR MULTIPLE USE

One of the most important decisions to make is whether the space intended for music performance also will be used for drama. Space to be used only for concerts involves far fewer design compromises. However, performance areas for music alone should not be planned if a space does not exist elsewhere for play production. In this instance, lighting, rigging, scenery-handling equipment, and other building elements necessary for drama are thrust into the planning process too late to be assimilated properly. This can leave the drama staff without facilities or with ones that provide an inhospitable environment. The results can also be bad for musicians for the late introduction of production elements (or adding them after construction is completed), often hampers all activities. If a multi-use space is needed, it is better to establish this fact early and design it accordingly.

School auditoriums seldom are built for a single purpose. As schools consolidate, specialized facilities like the auditorium move toward serving the entire system or community. Progressive planners accept the broad concept of shared school and community use, particularly for libraries, gymnasiums, and auditoriums. This approach makes a multipurpose auditorium essential, and it must be designed for as much flexibility and adaptability as possible. The planning team should minimize any conflicts between acoustical requirements and audience/performer relationships. The ideal solution, of course, is to have separate spaces for music and drama. A small theater is a desirable supplement to a large auditorium, especially if enrollments and activity can support both facilities. Even small institutions should have a flexible room for theatrical experimentation and production in addition to the large auditorium. The need for this kind of space relates more to the creativity and activity of the drama department than to the size of the institution or the community.

USES OF THE AUDITORIUM

If the auditorium is to serve many functions, a list of common uses can be a helpful guide. The estimated frequency of each use also can be valuable to the planner. If compromises in design cannot be avoided, they should be made to favor the most frequent uses.

A combined school/community auditorium might be used for the following:
- Band, orchestra, and choir concerts
- Solo recitals and chamber music programs
- Musicals, operettas, or operas
- Combined music festivals and concerts

Figure 1. Ideal auditorium size for various presentations

Seating capacity	Performance area	Most successful presentations	State design and audience configuration
100 to 200	200 to 400 square feet	Recital, small ensemble, experimental drama, lecture, film	Flexible
300 to 500	350 to 600 square feet	Recital, chamber music, choir, drama, lecture, film	Flexible
600 to 1,000	600 to 1,000 square feet	All of the above, plus small orchestra and ballet (dance)	Open stage, semithrust, or modified proscenium; audience usually on one floor, but for 1,000 seats there may be one balcony
1,300 to 1,800	2,000 square feet plus side stages	Orchestra, band, choir, opera, ballet, drama, lyric theater (drama with some sound reinforcement)	Open stage, semithrust, or modified proscenium; concert shell for music; one balcony
2,000 to 2,400	2,000 square feet plus side stages	All of those listed immediately above (drama and musical theater require full sound reinforcement)	Open stage, modified proscenium, proscenium with concert shell; two balconies
2,500 to 3,000	over 2,000 square feet	Symphonic band (full sound system dependence for other events)	Open stage, modified proscenium, proscenium with concert shell; two to three balconies
over 3,000	over 2,500 square feet	Film, projected television, band, orchestra, choir (all performances require full sound system)	Proscenium stage, arenas, stadiums, etc.; two to three balconies; very long viewing distances

- Popular, folk, or rock music
- Ballet
- Assemblies and lectures
- Dramatic productions
- Conferences and workshops
- Movies and travelogues

Some presentations may be by students or by visiting professionals. The latter will have some requirements not otherwise needed in a purely educational situation, such as separate dressing rooms and possibly special stage and lighting needs.

SEATING CAPACITY

The audience/performer relationship, room shape, and room size all affect seating capacity, and the reverse is equally true. In actual practice, the audience area and stage must be designed together. Sight lines for the audience are determined by the height of the stage floor and the width of the stage. The placement of masking devices for stage lighting and offstage areas depends on the location of the seats. The number of seats is interrelated with these and several other factors. In a commercial theater and in certain other specific situations, it may be desirable to accommodate an entire potential attendance at one performance. In an educational situation, however, there are many cogent arguments for keeping the auditorium small. When a fine program is prepared, there may be value in having repeat performances. From this viewpoint, it might be practical to reduce the seating capacity of the auditorium or theater and to spend the funds for better equipment so the performances can be presented adequately.

A small hall enhances the interplay between the performer and the audience by making facial expressions and other nuances more perceptible. This is especially important for drama performances, as success tends to be measured in inverse proportion to the distance of the audience from the stage. It is also helpful for choral concerts, chamber music programs, and solo recitals. From an acoustical aspect, seating capacity (which determines seating area) is so critical that once the size of the audience area is set, many of the acoustical parameters also are established. Each size auditorium has its own character and feeling. Some kinds of performances are optimized in halls of a certain size while others are compromised. Problems arise most frequently in halls that are too large or too small and that lack flexibility in form. The chart shown in figure one summarizes the relationship between auditorium size and function and points to those combinations that yield the best results.

When trying to decide the size of a new auditorium, many planners have found it useful to make a study of actual audience size at previous events. An estimate of how many evenings a year the largest audience would attend is helpful in determining whether the high cost of providing space for such an audience is justified. This information, in addition to a careful review of future day-to-day needs, is essential to intelligent planning. If only a few large productions a year are presented, a gymnasium, field house, or community center may have to serve as best it can, leaving the smaller auditorium to serve ideally the many other events. Giving a concert to a "standing room only" audience in a smaller auditorium is certainly more satisfying than playing to a half-empty house in a huge hall. The educational goals of the orchestra, band, or choir are achieved as well if not better in such circumstances.

SEATING ARRANGEMENTS

Continental seating

One of the decisions to be made in considering how to accommodate the audience is whether the seats will be installed in unbroken rows with no rear-to-front aisles within the seating area, or in the more traditional method with two or three aisles. In

Left: Kansas City Music Hall. Conventional seating includes several front-to-back aisles in the audience area, with no more than fourteen seats between aisles.
Below: Davies Symphony Hall, San Francisco, California. Continental seating allows the performer to face an unbroken audience area. Photographs by Irwin Seating Company.

Europe, the former arrangement is quite common; hence, the term "continental seating" is used to designate aisle-less seating. The advantage of this type is that the performer faces an unbroken audience area; where a center aisle once would have been, one now finds the best seats in the house. To permit convenient entry to the middle seats, the rows are placed far enough apart to permit patrons to slide past occupied seats easily. Better seating arrangements result without the arbitrary confinements of the code-regimented aisle seating arrangements. Rows are usually spaced no less than thirty-nine to forty-two inches apart from back to back. Many new concert halls and opera houses in the United States and Canada as well as a number of school and college auditoriums have adopted this seating system. Some halls have seats that push back a few inches to increase clearance, making a back-to-back dimension of thirty-eight inches acceptable. Exit doors must be provided every five rows or every twenty-five feet along the side. Audience-circulating patterns and lobby areas at the rear or sides are considerably different from those for conventional seating arrangements.

Conventional seating

The traditional practice of a back-to-front aisle still is desirable for many school auditoriums. Rows may be placed comfortably thirty-six to thirty-seven inches apart from back to back, there is less possible friction between students, and teacher's access to the center seats is more convenient. The aisle space may offer an acoustical advantage if it provides a hard, reflective area that is unobstructed even when the house is full. With fewer seats between aisles, there is apt to be less foot trampling by latecomers. Conventional seating should be used in balconies, in halls more than sixty seats wide, and in halls with very steeply terraced seating areas.

Flexible spaces for seating

A caliper stage is one that extends around part of the sides of the audience area. In a nonproscenium house, it can be adapted as a supplementary seating area for the audience. For this purpose, chairs should offer some of the amenities of regular audience seating, with padding and contours for comfort rather than posture. Seating should not get so close to the performers that they become uneasy. Precautions may be needed to ensure safety if there is a sizable drop to the auditorium floor. Access aisles must be maintained.

Another flexible area for seating is the orchestra pit. If the pit is operable, the front should be made in removable sections so that, with the pit floor at audience level, portable seating may be installed for special occasions. This seating can match the regular seats by being mounted on carts that lock into place, or they may (like the caliper chairs) stack or fold. A pit for a fifty-piece orchestra with the railing removed can accommodate another one hundred audience members.

OTHER SEATING CONSIDERATIONS

Options such as retractable seats, perforated seat bottoms, and aisle or under-seat carpeting must be chosen on the basis of the requirements and design concepts of the individual project. However, if the auditorium is to serve all its users well, these decisions must first accede to acoustical considerations.

DIVIDED AUDITORIUMS

During the 1950s, planners were quick to recommend subdivided auditorium configurations as a way to justify expenditures of tax money on classrooms rather than for seldom-used auditoriums. Federal funding further served to encourage the divisibility concept; in fact, a number of quite good facilities were built and stand today as examples of careful design and construction. However, even the best of these facilities has been forced to live with compromises that would not have existed

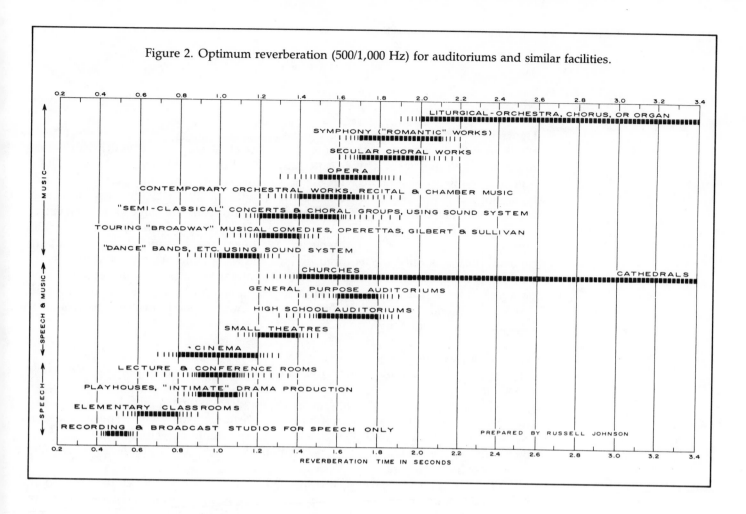

Figure 2. Optimum reverberation (500/1,000 Hz) for auditoriums and similar facilities.

in undivided auditoriums. Subdividing is costly in terms of equipment and in its waste of expensive building area. It adds unnecessary square footage in auditorium spaces (which always are built at premium cost) to provide for teaching positions that require otherwise unnecessary access space and that are less expensive elsewhere. The increased area degrades viewing conditions, substantially increases viewing distances, and results in impaired acoustics. Better facilities can be built more efficiently and at lower cost if separated, with classrooms built as classrooms and auditoriums built as auditoriums. The considerably increased community use of the auditorium that invariably follows the opening of a new hall easily provides the price justification formerly sought by combining classrooms within the auditorium.

ACOUSTICAL REQUIREMENTS

Optimum environments for the varied activities in an auditorium are not the same. While there are other acoustical factors to be considered, the most important is the reverberation time at middle frequencies, which is calculated according to an established formula. It requires instruments for accurate measurement, or it can be figured from blueprints in advance. Speech and drama require about one second, while music requires reverberation times of one and one-half to two seconds or more, depending on the space and the performance (see figure 2). For speech, the listener wants most of the sound to arrive directly from the source, whereas for music, total envelopment by the sound is desirable. These conflicting requirements can be met by incorporating adjustable acoustical devices into the hall or auditorium. Without them, one or more of the uses will be compromised considerably.

STAGE

Doors

All doors entering on a stage must be of sufficient height and width to provide ready access to the stage. This is especially true of the scenery doors. They must be high enough to accommodate wide stage wagons, large instruments, and occasionally, motor vehicles. The doors for scenery should be at least eight feet wide and fourteen feet tall, and all other doors leading to and from the stage should be extra-wide double doors. All exterior doors leading into the auditorium should be solid, without windows, and mounted securely. All doors must operate silently. Panic bars on exit doors generally are required by law, but sometimes are rendered useless by padlocks and chains. This is an extremely dangerous practice. Doors should be gasketed to prevent a bypassing of the sound isolation construction, and threshold drop seals should be provided. Every attempt must be made to keep the sound of heavy rain or thunder from penetrating into the auditorium.

Apron and calipers

Caliper stage extensions around the sides of the audience area provide interesting possibilities for antiphonal music performances, overflow capabilities for large groups, and supplementary acting areas for the drama department. For concert use, the open floor area of the calipers enhances the acoustics somewhat. The stage apron should be wide enough that pianos and other equipment can be used in front of the main curtain. For certain musical performances, it may be advisable to extend the apron over the orchestra pit.

The floor of the stage proper, if combined for music/theater/dance use, should be white pine tongue-and-groove lumber with plywood subflooring laid on sleepers and resilient pads. The floor should be stained a very dark brown—almost black—and one coat of nongloss sealer applied. Linoleum, hardboard, or other decks can be laid on this floor for special purposes. Both sides of the stage should be provided with fixed or portable steps. These steps should be wide enough so musical instruments and other small properties can be carried from the auditorium to the stage, or to allow students to approach the stage two abreast.

Chairs and risers

Chairs for the stage should be specified in sufficient quantity to be readily at hand for rehearsals and other stage uses. Stacking chairs stored on portable racks take up a minimum of backstage room and yet are moved easily.

Portable risers should be provided as part of regular stage equipment. For music performances, these include stepped risers for seated band, orchestra, or chorus, as well as a set of risers for the standing choir. Four- by six-foot folding platforms with wheels provide ease of movement and set up and can be used for both music and drama performances. They are available in eight-inch heights, with increments of eight inches up to thirty-two or forty inches if desired. Storage space for risers and chairs convenient to the stage should be provided. Hydraulically operated stage sections can be included for drama use. However, these are expensive and may receive too little use to justify their inclusion. Homemade risers, as compared to factory-built, present a safety and liability hazard that rule them out for school use. Riser manufacturers have specially designed hardware and have carefully tested their products with a built-in safety factor that is hard to match.

Lighting

There are many concepts in stage lighting, whether the facility to be lighted is a proscenium theater, an open stage, or a modified proscenium. The border and footlight installations once popular in school auditoriums are no longer considered

adequate. In addition to sufficient downlights for concerts and other nontheatrical presentations, school auditoriums need stage lighting for musicals and drama productions. The amount of lighting and the type required depends on the design of the auditorium and the nature of the productions (see chapter four).

Front lighting from slots in the auditorium ceiling (serviced by catwalks) is highly desirable. Additional wall slots and a location for a follow spot in the rear of the auditorium are common. Spotlights are needed on battens, stands, or tormentor pipes to provide further illumination of the stage. Border lights and sometimes footlights are used for toning and blending. Beam lights are used for backlighting. Floodlights are used for background effects, and special footlights are needed for a cyclorama. Side lighting sometimes is provided by spotlights from a mobile tower in the wings. An elaborate college or community theater installation may include a light bridge. Open stages and modified proscenium stages frequently use projected backgrounds. The lamp housing for scenic projection may be located on a catwalk above the stage area or in a ceiling slot above the front curtain.

The stage lighting control board should be located at the rear of the auditorium in a lighting booth. In addition to operable windows and an intercom phone, monitor loudspeakers also are needed so the operator can hear what is going on in the auditorium if the windows are closed during a performance. Switchboard facilities should service an adequate number of floor pockets, which will vary with the size of the auditorium, stage, and its lighting equipment. A dimmer system must be part of the lighting installation.

There can never be too many outlets. It is better to have many adequate outlets than to risk overloading a few. Normally, there should be three or four locations for floor pockets across both the right and left sides of the stage, across the back of the stage, and on each side of the acting area. Each pocket should be capable of handling three to six 3,000-watt circuits. All wiring for stage lights must be kept off the floor. This sometimes is accomplished by using overhead flexible drops to service the ladders or towers. Tormentor lights are serviced from proscenium pockets. Auditorium and proscenium slots are serviced from standard stage pockets located within the slots.

Rigging

This book does not treat rigging systems or other drama-associated aspects of spaces shared by the two arts. On these matters consultants should be called in.

Cyclorama

It was once thought that every school stage was adequately furnished if it had a cyclorama—a continuous curtain around the sides and rear of the stage. Since this curtain usually was made of heavy velour, its effect on stage acoustics (when used for music) was detrimental. Every attempt should be made to avoid heavy draperies that deaden the stage and destroy the acoustical matching of the stage to the house. If

Left: Portable stages with folding legs are easy to set up indoors or outdoors and take a minimum of storage space. Photograph by Wenger Corporation.
Right: The stage lighting control board should be located at the rear of the auditorium in a booth overlooking the stage. The sound control console should be in the audience seating area and open to the loudspeaker system.

absorbent curtains are used, they should retract into pockets, but this will not be practical unless the exposed rear stage wall presents an acceptable visual background for concerts and theater. The rear wall should be made of wood, troweled block, brick, or concrete block. It should not be painted white or near-white, since light-colored surfaces make it difficult for the performers to see. If there is a surface pattern, the director may want to use the cyclorama to cover the wall. The cyclorama should not be too light in color. In some situations, portable sound-reflecting panels and overhead, track-supported pivoting panels can combine the functions of side masking curtains and concert shell side walls. These, along with fixed reflectors, can be designed with the assistance of the acoustics and theater consultants. Using theatrical masking curtains, valences, and the cyclorama to mask catwalks, as well as a scenery fly loft and offstage areas will make a concert shell mandatory. The stage is one area where meeting the needs of both music and drama requires foresight and care in the planning. Figure three shows the rigging needed for a music/drama auditorium.

Orchestra/band shell

If the auditorium has a traditional proscenium stage, a shell must be used for music productions. Room for shell storage also must be provided. The purpose of the shell is to project the sound into the audience for lectures, recitals, and concerts. It conserves acoustic energy and directs it out to the listeners. It enhances communication between performers, increases dynamic range, and improves tone quality and blend. The acoustical shell is discussed in greater detail in chapter four.

Budgeting for equipment

Nowhere in a music facility is there likely to be so much latitude in the type and cost of equipment as there is for the stage. Unfortunately, there have been many projects in which an auditorium and stage have been planned without adequate budgeting for the needed stage systems. These are major expense items that should be accepted from the beginning. Stage systems requiring special design and budgetary consideration are: theater lighting, controls, and instruments; stage rigging; stage curtains and sound-reflecting panels; a band/orchestra/choir acoustical shell; the orchestra pit (stage lift); sound system and recording; and projection equipment. An experienced theater consultant can provide budget figures for these systems. Provisions should be made for the correct equipment at the start instead of adding it at a later time, since it will invariably cost more, and will lead to unresolvable compromises that add-on systems always bring about.

Figure 3. Stage-rigging system for a music/drama auditorium	
Rigging required for	**Remarks**
Safety curtains	Required only in proscenium spaces; may be omitted in certain instances, such as when a flood system is included (check fire code)
Light battens	Required only in proscenium spaces (catwalks take the place of battens in open stage spaces)
Concert shell	Required only in proscenium spaces; motorized battens desirable; often only shell ceiling is flown
Lightbridges and heavy weights	Motorized battens are best
Cyclorama and stage pieces	Required only in proscenium spaces; counterweight line sets and other rope sets are essential (rope sets not required in open-stage performance spaces, but they do add flexibility)

Center for the Arts, University of Wisconsin in Plattville. An acoustical shell is essential for effective music performance on a proscenium stage. Acoustics: Artec Consultants.

Offstage areas

Connected ancillary spaces to the stage must provide adequate storage for stage sets, sound panels, stage risers, music racks, and other materials and equipment connected with concert and drama presentations. The special backstage facilities needed for drama—scene shop, costume shop, properties room, rehearsal rooms, green rooms, special dressing rooms, and other areas—are outside the scope of this book. In a multipurpose auditorium, however, careful planning of proper storage facilities is especially important so that changeovers from music to drama are simplified. Music ensembles and drama groups may need access to the stage during the same time periods. Orderly and sufficient storage space close to the stage will help ease scheduling conflicts and promote efficient use of the auditorium.

Orchestra pit

Musical theater and opera represent an acoustically difficult marriage of instruments and voices. Particularly in educational and semiprofessional performances, instrumental sound tends to overwhelm voices. The orchestra pit must receive particularly careful acoustical design of each element to help overcome the balance problems inherent in these situations. Closed-circuit television and creative scenery design can open other performing locations for the orchestra. However, the orchestra pit remains the most suitable location, and every auditorium that hopes to accommodate music theater, ballet, or opera should include one. The critical parameters in pit design are area, configuration, and treatment.

Fifteen square feet per musician is a reasonable guide that assumes performing groups of greater than twenty-five musicians, including piano and percussion. For any facility that is to accommodate opera or ballet, a pit area of no less than 1,000 square feet should be provided. This will accommodate sixty to seventy-five musicians, depending on instrumentation.

In order for the conductor to see and be seen by both pit musicians and onstage performers, the depth of the pit must be no greater than seven and one-half feet to eight feet below stage level. To achieve an adequate area for musicians (while not

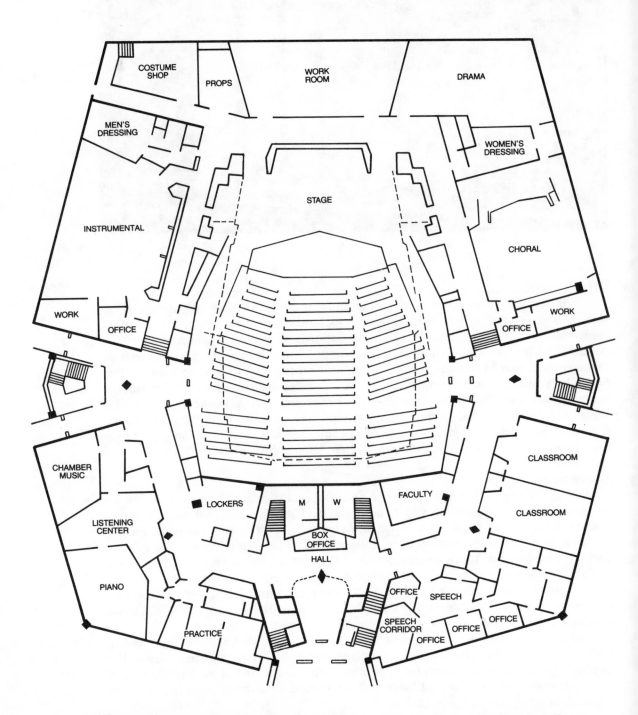

Calvin College Fine Arts Center, Grand Rapids, Michigan. Corridors, drinking fountains and other facilities can be located to serve the students during the day and the audience in the evening. Architects: The Perkins & Will Partnership, Daverman Associates.

cutting too deeply into the audience area), the space under the stage apron frequently is used. This space should not exceed six feet in depth and should have a height of six and one-half feet clear. This implies that the thickness of the stage floor overhanging the pit should not exceed twelve inches. A length-to-width ratio of 2:1 or less is desirable to maintain reasonable balance and ensemble. The width of the opening should not be less than nine to ten feet, nor the length greater than fifty-five to sixty feet. If at all possible, the orchestra pit platform should be mechanized.

Controlling the loudness of the pit orchestra while maintaining well-balanced sound projection presents a sensitive design problem. Since the upstage wall of the pit acts as an acoustic mirror reflecting sound to the audience, covering it with adjustable or permanent sound-absorbing material considerably diminishes the loudness perceived by an audience on the main floor. To the extent that the performers are more visible, listeners in the balcony experience less change with this treatment than those on the main floor.

A railing with solid infill, all or part of which can be removed, is required on the audience side of the pit to shield the first few rows of listeners from being overwhelmed by pit sound. The railing further serves to aid communication by reflecting pit sound to onstage performers. Absorptive material should not be installed on this wall. Additional loudness control can be achieved (and some blending and fullness developed) by coupling the pit volume with the volume of a possible seating storage area located under the first few rows of audience seating. Coupling with a trap room under the stage (into which actors can "disappear" through a trap door in the stage floor) also may serve this function. In addition to these acoustical needs, there are many other factors that must be considered, including access from the pit to warm-up rooms, dressing rooms, and so forth; storing removable seating if the pit doubles as an audience seating area; storing pianos and percussion instruments; pit cover design if mechanization is not feasible; and use of the pit lift as a freight elevator that connects lower-level areas with the stage.

The orchestra pit should be tied into the house intercom system, with stations backstage and to the front of the house. Orchestral music stands have been designed that are large enough to hold unusual sizes of manuscript paper, and have built-in lights. The pit should have enough outlets installed in the floor and along the walls to accommodate a maximum-size orchestra. The circuits should be controlled from the stage lighting control board.

STAGE MANAGER'S DESK

Every well-equipped auditorium should include provisions for a stage manager. While some of the stage manager's functions can be performed from control areas in the rear of an auditorium, the job can be performed best from a portable reading desk. The stage manager must communicate with performers and other technicians and should be provided a wall-mounted panel containing a desk cable outlet, a telephone handset, an electrical outlet, and a large clock synchronized with the clock in the hall. The completely equipped stage manager's desk includes these features:

- Reading surface with retaining lip
- Dimmer-controlled reading light
- House telephone or intercom master station
- Paging master system
- Cueing master station (items three, four, and five can be combined into one system in less sophisticated installations)
- Pit lift controls
- Remote controls for concert, lecture, and house lights
- Panic lighting controls to throw on house lights in an emergency
- Backstage work light and rehearsal light control
- Electrical outlet

- Adjustable-height stool with foot rail
- Pencil sharpener
- Coffee cup retaining ring
- Locked drawer
- Thirty-foot interconnecting cable to wall panel (with means of coiling unused cable)

LOADING DOCK/RECEIVING ROOM

Each performance hall must have an accessible loading dock for receiving equipment with space for temporary holding. Desirable features of the receiving area are:
- Steps or a ramp for personnel access
- Roof overhang for bad weather loading
- Dock bumper for trucks
- Loading door, a minimum of eight feet wide and eight feet high
- At least three hundred square feet of receiving space
- Ramped or level access to backstage of the performance room, and to rehearsal, dressing, and stage storage rooms

PUBLIC FACILITIES

Public rooms

A common fault of school performing areas is that the lavatories and public rooms often are quite distant from the auditorium. In some instances, they are in parts of the building that are locked, so there can be no access to them during evening performances. The lounge facilities to accommodate the public between acts or during intermissions should be large enough for comfort. The ventilating system should be separated from that of the theater proper. An ideal and economical arrangement that works well is one in which corridors, drinking fountains, and other facilities serve the student body during the day and the audience at evening functions, thus eliminating the need for double facilities. Such multiple use should be kept in mind in locating areas that will serve the public, but it never should be achieved at the expense of other important considerations in a good layout. Signs should indicate clearly where the ticket office, public telephone, and other public facilities are located. Audiences at evening events are infrequent visitors compared to the students. A clear indication of the location of conveniences that are available is a matter of common courtesy that easily is overlooked. For audience recall after intermission, bells, chimes, a sound system to carry voice announcements, or a system for flashing lights in lobby areas should be provided.

Entrances and exits

Auditoriums must have adequate exits. The flow of pedestrian traffic to the ticket office, into the auditorium, and to or from parking facilities also must be considered. Cloakrooms should be convenient to building entrances, yet located where a line will not block exits or interfere with the orderly emptying of the auditorium.

Provision for handicapped persons

Those persons who attend public events in a wheelchair are now being given more consideration and recent building codes and federal standards have established guidelines that must be followed. It is wise to have the architect keep abreast of the latest requirements and assume responsibility that they are met. A few general current regulations can be stated for informal guidance. Ramps must be used instead of steps in at least one direct route to spaces for wheelchairs. These areas must have good line of sight, be an integral part of any fixed seating plan, and be dispersed throughout the seating area. An accessible route must also connect wheelchair seating locations with performance areas, including stages, dressing rooms, and other spaces used by performers.[5]

More specific requirements include:

- Provision of convenient parking with double-width spaces.
- Parking within 200 feet or less of the building entrance.
- Ramps twelve feet long for each rise of one foot to reach the entry level outside, or within the building if the level changes.
- Handrails thirty-one inches high and one and one-half inches from the wall on one side of each ramped passageway.
- Toilet facilities on each floor for each sex with spacing and heights from the floor that meet the special requirements.
- Water fountains, public telephones, controls, and switches at appropriately low levels above the floor.
- Space for two wheelchairs for each 100 seats in every performance area.

People with hearing handicaps should be provided with a wireless hearing assistance system with individual earphones and volume controls that they can use in any seating location. Units that use radio frequencies are very reliable, interference free, lower in cost, and are not limited by the line-of-sight coverage provided by infrared systems.

Tactile signs with raised or indented sans serif characters are required. Multistory buildings must have elevators, and parking areas have special location and dimensional requirements. Every effort should be made to meet or exceed current requirements to accommodate students as well as members of the audience who may be handicapped.

AUDITORIUM SAFETY

Recommended practice includes use of aisle and step lights whenever the hall is darkened for plays or movies. Exit lights are standard. Provisions for emergency lighting in case of power failure also must be included. A standby battery system is probably the least-expensive system that offers enough light for safety. Stage areas must be provided with automatic sprinklers in case of fire. The width of the aisles and the dimensions of the steps and risers are also safety considerations that come under the fire and building codes of each state or municipality. Onstage safety precautions, such as using steel (not rope) cables on all stage rigging, supplying safety lines, and installing rails on risers all are sensible. Public liability is a matter of concern to every school board or board of trustees operating a public auditorium. Contracts for nonschool use of the facilities must be drawn up carefully to require insurance by the user and absolve the school of any public liability. Such contracts should be drawn by the school attorney. The auditorium staff is expected to follow strict rules in maintaining uncluttered catwalks, security with safety chains, suspended panels, and lights, and effective emergency systems.

MANAGING THE AUDITORIUM

Teams planning an auditorium often fail to look ahead to its scheduling and actual operation. The auditorium is likely to be a busy place, and one individual may have responsibility for: maintaining a schedule book; contracting with nonschool users; invoicing and collecting for such uses; providing needed equipment and technical staff; overseeing adjustable features in a multipurpose auditorium; supervising maintenance; arranging for ushers, ticket-takers, and parking supervisors; and managing all other details that need to be handled properly for the hall to realize its full service potential. This is done best by having a building manager with an office convenient to both the public and the school, or by assigning these responsibilities to someone on the office staff.

5. See *Uniform Federal Accessibility Standards*, (Washington, D.C.: General Services Administration, 1984), 4–7.

The section on illumination and color found in chapter four was updated by C. Harold Barcus, professor of architecture at Miami University at Oxford, Ohio, where he has also been in private architectural practice since 1951 with the firm Barcus, Moore, Swirn, in Oxford.

TECHNICAL CONSIDERATIONS

(In using material in this chapter, it is suggested the reader also refer to the section on planning instructional areas found in pages 11–20.)

Designing a music facility is a specialized task that taxes the capabilities of the school staff as well as those of many architects. This is especially true in the area of technical considerations. Careful planning in this regard yields larger dividends than in any other aspect of the building process, and it is here that the specialized services of trained and experienced consultants can be used to best advantage.

When designing a music building, two basic technical problems must be faced. First, the various spaces must be adequately isolated for satisfactory simultaneous use. Second, satisfactory acoustics in each room must be provided. These two objectives are achieved by completely different mechanisms. Isolation is achieved by construction that separates two spaces while room acoustics are determined by room size, shape, and the kind of finishing materials used in the interior. There is a misconception, for example, that the addition of sound-absorbing curtains on a wall will improve the isolation of sound from an adjoining space. This will do nothing but deaden the room's acoustics, and will have very little effect on the amount of sound coming through from adjoining rooms.

SOUND ISOLATION

Sound isolation is the containment of sounds within the space where they are generated or keeping unwanted sounds out. The intrusion of external sounds or the noise of a ventilating system can neutralize all the advantages of carefully planned room acoustics. Noisy ventilating systems are the number one problem in both and new music buildings. Consequently, the requirements for effective sound containment (in mechanical systems) and sound-isolation should be given primary consideration.

The degree of sound isolation required in the music building will vary with their use. The most critical isolation problem is found in teaching studios and classrooms. Any audible musical sound is intelligible (as contrasted with speech, which transmits as a vague mumble). This is especially important in classrooms used for music dictation, where musical sound from an adjoining room can be distracting. Score reading and composition also require inaudibility of sounds from adjoining spaces. Practice rooms have less critical sound-isolation requirements, although even these will not be satisfactory unless more than the usual classroom separation is provided.

Large rehearsal rooms and recital halls often can be placed in separate units and thus can achieve the isolation they require. One could imagine a music building in which the isolation of all spaces could be achieved by widely separating all the rooms on a single level, but this is hardly practical. Spaces should be conveniently located, and ways must be found to provide the required isolation.

Effective sound isolation is achieved by constructing heavy, airtight walls, floors, and ceilings—the heavier the better. There is a limit, however, to how much isolation can be achieved in a typical building. No matter how heavy a wall is made, some sound will travel through the floor and ceiling to adjoining spaces on the same level. The isolation limit set by these flanking paths is too low for the critical spaces in a music building. More complex constructions than those usually satisfactory in classroom buildings are therefore mandatory. Very high levels of sound isolation in a concrete building can be achieved by floating an inner skin (walls, floors, and ceilings) for each of the spaces within the basic structure. The structure of the building must be protected from airborne and structure-borne sound waves by the addition of a resilient layer of plaster or concrete. A discussion of this complex type of structure with an architect almost always elicits the question, "Isn't there some simpler way of doing it?" The answer is, "Unfortunately, no." This type of floated interior construction also gives isolation from the structure-borne sounds of pianos, cellos, and other instruments that drive the floor directly.

The need for high sound isolation precludes the possibility of using natural ventilation. However, frequent air exchange and the introduction of fresh air are important in music rooms (especially in rehearsal rooms). A music building must be air-conditioned throughout, and air must be supplied through sound-absorbent, lined ductwork and returned through lined ductwork, possibly incorporating silencers if the lengths of ductwork between spaces are inadequate. Door louvers and other usual ventilation practices cannot be used. While the isolated interior skin of the room may be shaped to serve the purposes of good room acoustics, it must be heavy, continuous, and not short-circuited to the basic structure of the building by electrical conduits, ventilating ducts, or any other rigid path. The details of windows and doors are not easy, but they must be worked out in each case. These problems can be solved if the designer is willing to take the trouble. The investment in the added cost of construction will not be realized in adequate sound isolation, however, unless every single detail is considered in the design and is seen through carefully to completion. It is helpful to instruct workmen in the reasoning behind the fussy construction system and the necessity of avoiding any accidental bridges between the floated interior and the basic structure of the building. Even so, supervision by a knowledgeable person during the actual construction of these critical areas is imperative. A music building incorporating this specialized kind of construction will be as much as twice as expensive as a normal classroom building.

Practice rooms often can be treated more simply in terms of isolation, but they, too, require the supply and return of air through lined ductwork and weatherstripped doors (perhaps less expensive doors than those used in teaching studios and classrooms). This assumes that there will be some audibility of sound from an adjoining room when no sound is being made in a given room, but that it will not disturb a person who is practicing.

When this complex type of construction is used, there still may be some audible musical sound from the next space if the background sound level is very low. A moderate background noise level in teaching and practice spaces is acceptable and can even be helpful. The air conditioning system can provide a slightly audible air noise. In air-conditioning terms, this background noise may have a spectrum of NC30–35. (NC=Noise Criteria—a set of curves used to identify levels of sound at different frequencies.) Such background noise will not interfere with normal activities in teaching spaces and will effectively mask or conceal the tiny amounts of sound that

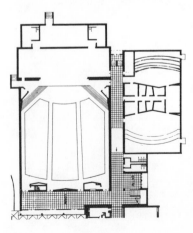

Large rehearsal rooms can be placed in separate units to achieve sound isolation.

inevitably intrude (with even the best construction). A masking background also can be useful in the music library to hide both speech and musical intrusions from other activities. Music listening rooms require the same construction as teaching studios, including the moderate continuous background noise. Because mechanical systems are at times unpredictable or erratic, it may be helpful to generate the masking sound electronically. Recital halls, auditoriums, and any spaces to be used for recording or music performance must be completely free of noise; absolutely no masking noise can be tolerated there.

No matter how effective the sound-isolating construction between spaces may be, the overall isolation achieved will be better if rehearsal rooms are not located over recital halls, or noisy mechanical equipment is not placed under the stage. Isolation can be achieved in such situations, but it always costs more than when these elements are separated. Single story, on-grade construction usually provides the most practical and least expensive isolation for music wings and always should be considered first.

Sound-absorbing treatments should be used in all corridors and lobbies to minimize the transmission of sound, and as many doors as possible should be closed between rooms to ensure isolation. No corridor treatment is as effective as a closed door. Doors to all isolated rooms must be of special sound-isolating construction, and they must be fully weatherstripped on all four sides. Any leaks or cracks (no matter how small) will nullify the effectiveness of the doors. The weatherstripping must be maintained and adjusted periodically to keep it airtight. Even the best acoustical doors available are not as effective in containing sound within a room as are well-designed and carefully constructed walls. Glass vision panels or glass wall panels can weaken the sound-isolating capabilities unless they are double-glazed with a deep airspace between, are properly installed, and are carefully sealed. In critical areas, they should be avoided.

Use of a sound lock at entrances to practice areas, rehearsal rooms, or auditoriums often is advisable. A sound lock consists of two separate doors with a vestibule between them. In an area devoted to practice rooms or teaching studios, it seldom is considered worthwhile to install two doors, even though single well-sealed doors still will permit appreciable sound transmission to the corridors. From one practice room to another, there always will be two doors in the path, and room-to-corridor isolation is not critical. But a word of caution is in order about the so-called "soundproof" or "acoustical" doors on the market. Test results always are based on ideal installations under laboratory conditions, and should not be taken too literally. Obviously, wood doors must be solid rather than hollow core. If compression-type gasketing systems are used, they must be very soft and easily compressed. Packages are available that include the doors and the gasketing system, and these tend to be more acceptable than separate ones. The desired performance must be specified carefully by the design team and not just designated as soundproof or weatherstripped. Drop seals tend to click and should be avoided in quiet performing spaces. Requiring performance specifications, in which tests of the complete installation are made by the acoustics consultant before the installation is accepted by the owner, will ensure satisfactory performance. Quality of installation is so important that such performance specifications may be the only way of ensuring adequate performance. Unless this is done, funds for special doors may be wasted.

ACOUSTICS

Attention to the acoustical environment is important in every building, but it must be particularly well handled in a music building. Without good conditions for performance, rehearsal, teaching, composing, or reading, a music building simply cannot provide the environment for good teaching. Acoustics, like structure, air conditioning, and lighting, must be considered from the very beginning of building planning. Unfortunately, there are no shortcuts to the achievement of satisfactory

Doors are the weakest element in a practice room, teaching/studio suite. They must be solid-core special acoustical doors, with no windows (or double-glazed if windows are absolutely necessary), adjustable special sound seals around the jambs and head and a threshold drop seal to make them airtight. They should never open directly into a rehearsal room if simultaneous use is expected.

Individual panels of absorbent materials covered with grill cloth can be hung from picture moldings to provide adjustable acoustics for studios and practice rooms.

conditions. It either *is* or *is not* a good music facility. Achieving satisfactory acoustics means more than providing a space free of obvious acoustic faults, and it is more than isolating sound from surrounding areas when sound is not wanted. The acoustic properties of a room can enhance the quality of music for the listener and can give the performers a sense of support that adds to the pleasure and quality of their performance.

ROOM ACOUSTICS

After the required isolation has been provided, it must be determined how these isolated spaces sound to their occupants. The acoustical problems in small practice rooms and even in medium or large rehearsal rooms are quite different from those in large recital halls and auditoriums: It is impossible to make them sound alike, as architects are often asked to do. The acoustics of a good auditorium enhance the beauty and balance of the sound. A good rehearsal room in an educational facility, on the other hand, is designed to fulfill its function best as a teaching station; clarity and focus on individuals are important if precision, intonation, and other fundamentals of musicianship are to be analyzed and improved. This work is carried on more effectively in a well-designed rehearsal room than in a reverberant auditorium. For musicians with a high degree of proficiency, this factor is less important, but is nevertheless a relevant consideration at the school and college level.

Spaces that vary in size will vary in sound, and their treatments must differ accordingly. An undertreated small room can be loud, harsh, muddy, and quite unacceptable for any music uses. The reverberation time in a small studio must be considerably lower than that considered ideal in a large rehearsal room. Because sound travels at the same speed in all spaces, the separation between successive reflections of sound becomes greater in larger rooms.

In a small practice room or teaching studio, there are stronger resonant frequencies in the audible range that must be suppressed. In some cases, the control of these resonances may require that the room have certain dimensional proportions. In larger rooms, where the predominant resonances are at subaudible frequencies, proportions

Irregular wall surfaces help to disperse sound in the auditorium.

become less important than basic requirement for height and width. Sound-absorbing materials in a small music room generally are required on at least two adjacent walls and the ceiling. These materials should be effective throughout the full frequency range. Acoustic tile that is glued to a ceiling is not as effective in the low and middle frequency ranges as is a suspended laid-in system. For reverberation control, either a sound-absorbing ceiling or fully carpeted floor can be incorporated. A curtain track along the wall allows heavy draperies to be either extended across the wall or pushed back into the corner to vary the reverberant characteristics of the space. These are matters of individual taste and preference, and one cannot predict in advance what an individual is likely to prefer. Because of this, a flexible acoustical system may be incorporated into practice rooms and teaching studios. Special one-inch picture moldings are installed on all the walls, and individual panels of absorptive material can be hung from them. These panels can be made inexpensively in a school shop out of two- by four-inch lumber filled with fiberglass sheets and covered with fabric. Thus, each studio can be custom-treated to suit the requirements of each teacher and each space. Some on-the-spot experimenting over a period of time is then possible. A hard-finished small room will not be liked by anyone, and a room completely padded with sound-absorbing material also is unlikely to be appreciated.

Flutter echo or ring, caused by the reflection of sound back and forth between parallel surfaces, can be avoided by installing absorptive treatments to eliminate hard opposing parallel surfaces or by avoiding the parallelism itself. It can be avoided either by skewing or tilting of the walls, or by added devices as tilted blackboards, bookcases filled with many objects, or wall surfaces with large design irregularities. Almost any architectural device that destroys the smooth parallelism between two wall surfaces will eliminate flutter echo.[6]

Whether the room is finished in plaster or wood is a matter of individual preference, and a wide variation of treatments can produce acceptable results. Small practice rooms and studios can be made comfortable to the occupant, and exterior

---

6. Further information on solving common acoustical problems can be found in the Appendix, page 134.

Western Michigan University, Kalamazoo, Michigan. Organ studios require special acoustical consideration.

windows here are acceptable. The prefabricated practice rooms mentioned in chapter two incorporate all required acoustic treatments.

ORGAN STUDIOS

Rooms for teaching or practicing the organ call for special consideration unless they are for the small electronic instruments that can be accommodated satisfactorily in a regular practice room. Pipe organs are found in increasing numbers in college studios. The first consideration in planning must be the physical size of the instrument. Organ consoles, pipework, chests, and action vary considerably, and many of them require more space than is found in a piano practice room. For acoustical reasons, the organ studio should be large enough to provide the instrument with space to speak out properly. It should be hard-surfaced, but with some acoustical flexibility so the organist can adjust the dryness or reverberance of the room. The larger the volume given to the instrument, the better. If scheduling permits, the planner even may consider placing the practice instruments in music classrooms to take advantage of the volume available.

CLASSROOMS

Large classrooms do not have the problem of low-frequency resonance because the principal resonances will be below the audible range. It still is important, however, to avoid flutter echoes between parallel wall surfaces and to control the reverberation time with adequate treatment of wall and ceiling surfaces. Fairly extensive treatments are needed to ensure that the low-frequency reverberation is not too long, but that there is still some life in the room to enhance the quality of musical sound. Placing acoustical tile on the entire ceiling (as is done in other classrooms), is not conducive to the best sound for music teaching. The ratio of reflective to absorptive material depends on the size and shape of the room, among other factors, and is best left to the judgment of the acoustical consultant.

REHEARSAL AREAS

Large rehearsal rooms for instrumental groups and for choruses often suffer from inadequate volume. A large instrumental rehearsal room should have a two-story ceiling of at least twenty-two to twenty-five feet for satisfactory conditions. Here, as in the teaching studios and classrooms, parallel hard wall surfaces should be avoided. The sound-absorbing treatment needed to control reverberation can be incorporated in the wall areas to help achieve this dispersion. The ceiling should have a mixture of sound-absorbing and sound-reflecting surfaces to enable the musicians to hear each other. Rehearsal rooms should not be too reverberant in order that the faulty performers can be identified and correctly readily. As in teaching studios, large areas of heavy draperies sometimes are provided for extension across one or two walls to vary the characteristics of the room. It also will make the room better serve the needs of both band and orchestra, since a more reverberant room is needed for orchestra rehearsal than for band. The installation of the curtain, which is most effective if made of heavy velour with a special liner, should be included in the original building budget.

Using carpeting in rehearsal rooms (see chapter two) does little if anything to counter the loudness and "boominess" that are the greatest threats to good rehearsal room sound. These factors are better controlled by fixed sound-absorbing treatment of much greater depth than carpeting provides. Placing absorption so close to the performer is unnatural and encourages forced tone production. Placing carpet under the percussion section to reduce its sound level makes some sense, as does sound-absorbing treatment close to them on the walls. But most players will hear themselves and the other performers better on a hard, reflective floor surface.

Good sound distribution is as important as reverberation time in a rehearsal room,

Southside Community Center, Elmira, New York. Large areas of heavy drapes on at least two adjacent walls provide acoustical adjustability in rehearsal rooms shared by band and choir or band and orchestra. Architect: Fanning, Howey Associates. Photograph by Gil Amiaga.

Kretschmer Recital Hall, Aquinas College, Grand Rapids, Michigan. An open stage recital hall provides an ideal acoustical environment for solo and small ensemble performances. Architect: Alfred Liu and Associates. Acoustics: Geerdes Consulting Services.

but it is a factor that often is minimized in the design. So is the need for broad-band sound absorption—not just that provided by carpeting or glued-on ceiling tile (both of which have little value in giving the room a flat response that is free of "boominess"). A wide variety of solutions is available to the architect, and the treatment selected will depend on the budget, the needs of the individual situation, and the expertise of the acoustical adviser. If the rehearsal room is to be used for some recording purposes, good acoustics, quiet lighting and ventilating systems, and enough volume for good musical sound become critical design considerations, although rehearsal rooms generally are too dead for serious recording.

RECITAL HALLS

The recital hall generally seats from 150 to 300 people and is used both for performances and rehearsals. The recital hall should have an adequate ceiling height to provide the volume required for proper reverberation time. If an organ is used, it may be desirable to provide heavy draperies to lower the reverberation time for piano and other instruments requiring less live space. The chairs in the recital hall always should be upholstered (never vinyl) to give a reasonably constant reverberation time regardless of occupancy. The hall should be more or less rectangular; circular halls should be avoided. The walls and ceiling surfaces should provide a high degree of sound diffusion through irregularities. The stage area, in particular, should be designed for good reflection of sound to the audience as well as to other performers on stage. The ceiling height above the performing platform should not exceed twenty feet—though it can be a little less—and the walls surrounding the platform should be skewed to avoid parallelism. Some people express a prejudice for using wood as the finish treatment in such a hall, but equally satisfactory results can be had with plaster. The old-fashioned rococo rooms with heavily coffered ceilings, walls treated with niches, statuary, and irregularities inevitably resulted in good sound. New ways must be found within a contemporary idiom to achieve these results. There should not be any background noise from the air conditioning system or from other spaces. Here, a masking noise would reduce audibility of sound. Constructing a quiet air-conditioning system is not easy, but it can be done.

AUDITORIUMS

The large auditorium, whether it is designed purely as a concert hall or as a multipurpose auditorium, poses problems considerably more difficult than those of small rehearsal rooms or recital halls. If its proposed uses indicate that fairly long reverberation times (two seconds) are desirable (as for organ and choral music), this will require a rather large volume for the space. Such an auditorium should not be larger than 1,500 or 2,000 seats. Although larger successful auditoriums have been built, the problems of achieving satisfactory acoustics become much greater, and their solutions require costly treatment that usually is not justified in educational situations.

Various seating arrangements for the audience have been discussed in chapter three. Fortunately, good sight lines also mean good hearing lines, and a steeply raked floor is helpful to good sound as well as sight. Deep underbalcony spaces must be avoided, and every listener must be able not only to see the performers, but must receive reflective sound from the upper wall and ceiling area. Careful balancing of sight line and acoustic requirements determines the seating geometry, which in turn determines the gross volume of the space for the achievement of the desired reverberation time. Also important, it also will determine the reflections needed from various surfaces in the hall to achieve intimacy and clarity as well as overall fullness and warmth.

Inevitably, the main ceiling of the auditorium is positioned high over the forward section of seating. This makes it necessary to add other reflecting surfaces at a lower height to give the required intimacy and clarity that come from early reflection of sound to the listener. The balance between the amount of early sound (that received directly from the source and from reflections within the first thirty or forty milliseconds after the original sound arrives at the ear) and the reverberant field that gives a sense of fullness and warmth must be worked out carefully. If there is too much early sound, there may not be enough body. Conversely, if there is not enough early sound, the result will lack definition and clarity. A good balance can be achieved, but its attainment will dictate the use of certain architectural details in the overall design of the auditorium.

GYMNASIUMS

A discussion of music performance areas should not have to include any rooms that compromise performance. However, many educational institutions, especially elementary schools do not have an auditorium. In these schools, music departments must make all of their public presentations in the school athletic facility. Most gymnasiums, because of their large volume and hard, reflective surfaces, are excessively muddy and "boomy," and their stages invariably are inadequate. Lighting designed for catching basketballs seldom is fit for reading sixteenth notes, and provisions for special stage lighting or for dimming audience circuits usually are not made. The audience also does not have customary amenities such as comfortable seating. Noisy ventilating systems commonly must be turned off during concerts, which promotes the discomfort of both performers and listeners.

In spite of this, many music festivals and concert performances are conducted each year in such inadequate spaces. The director who is faced with this unpleasant reality should make the best of it and not just accept the status quo. Even with considerable attention to acoustics, lighting, and so forth, playing or singing in a gymnasium never will equal performance in a good auditorium. However, it often can be made less intolerable if the problems encountered are analyzed and an attempt is made to minimize them. If an inadequate stage makes performance on the gymnasium floor necessary, a portable acoustic shell and portable staging (which is helpful for acoustical as well as visual reasons) will enhance the performance considerably, particularly if the ceiling and some side walls have tectum or other sound-absorbing materials on them. A cantilevered shell with built-in down lights provides lighting similar to that of an auditorium stage and also offers better sound reflection than the smaller, portable music shell. Acoustic consultants can help plan not only a new gymnasium, but also can help make an existing one less hostile for music.

SHELLS

Unless it has an open stage, a multipurpose hall rarely can serve music well without an acoustical enclosure. This is a fundamental requirement that must receive careful attention in the early planning and budgeting. Finding the expertise and the money to provide a proper shell later usually is nearly impossible. Thousands of performances each year are given in auditoriums built without this basic provision for staging concerts. Performers and listeners will never realize their full potential in a such areas.

A stage enclosure is an essential part of a multipurpose auditorium that has any kind of stage house. It cannot be considered a piece of optional stage equipment without disastrous results to any kind of music performance. No music organization can perform effectively on a stage draped with velour. The musicians simply will not be able to hear themselves (or each other), the projection of the sound to the audience will be inadequate, and if the hall is a live one acoustically, the onstage and offstage sounds will be completely different. The first requirement for good auditorium acoustics is an appropriate coupling of sound qualities on the sending end and the receiving end (see figure 4).

Design criteria for the shell must grow out of the musical requirements of the

World Theatre, St. Paul, Minnesota. A stage enclosure is an essential part of any music performance hall with a proscenium stage. Photograph by Wenger Corporation.

performers who will use the facility and the characteristics of the facility itself. If it is to serve the community symphony orchestra, the shell should be as sophisticated as the community can afford. For school use, the design should not be compromised severely if the best musical results are desired, but there are cost-cutting approaches that still will produce satisfactory results. Acoustical design considerations include energy conservation (to overcome losses due to sound absorption and sound transmission), onstage balance (to equalize upstage/downstage levels and improve intercommunication), general size, and configuration. Additionally, there are theatrical factors that influence the design of an enclosure, including construction methods and materials, operation and mobility, storage and maintenance, lighting, and safety.

If a shell is added to an existing auditorium, light battens may fall between ceiling panels. In some cases, this may be desirable in a new auditorium. Generally, however, the shell should not attempt to use border lights but should have lights installed in each section of the ceiling so that the stage will be flooded with a minimum of seventy footcandles of lighting. The lights should be arranged so that the back row will have sufficient light, and should be angled 15° to 18° so the lights will not throw a glare back into the audience. Front lighting may be used for fill only. The shell should be the full width of the proscenium. The ceiling can hang from the battens. The size of the shell can be varied by adding or subtracting flats and adding or subtracting ceiling sections. Its design should be entrusted to the acoustical consultant.

When an enclosure is provided, it should be designed so it can be erected and removed simply and quickly. This almost always means mechanization of the handling system, although some manually operated enclosures have given good results. The enclosure in a stagehouse should be fairly tight, with a minimum of openings to the backstage area. It should have sound diffusing surfaces and, if possible, some of these should be adjustable to permit various arrangements of performing groups and balance between sections. If the ceiling is more than twenty-five feet above the performers, there may be difficulty in onstage hearing. There are no miracle materials for enclosures. As in the case of sound isolation, the weight of the enclosure material will determine its reflectivity to the full sound spectrum.

A variation in auditorium design that permits music performances without having a stage enclosure is one in which the ensemble performs in the front part of the hall before a hard backdrop (usually an asbestos curtain or a special sound-reflecting screen) and uses the forward part of the auditorium walls and ceiling as its reflectors. This means that the capacity of the auditorium is reduced when used for orchestral performances, but it does minimize the amount of backstage setup work required to give the musicians a good performing environment.

An enclosure or shell also is required whenever music is performed outdoors. The same general principles govern the design of these outdoor enclosures. The once-popular semicircular or parabolic forms for these shells never should be used. Any form of concave geometry will focus certain sections of the performing group toward certain parts of the audience in an undesirable way.

An orchestra enclosure always should be made of surfaces with modulations to encourage sound diffusion and more uniform distribution. The exact shape of such an enclosure is determined by the geometry of the seating area as well as the size and nature of the performing groups. The greater the extension of the enclosure's ceiling out over the audience, the better the result. Shells can be built of wood, concrete, steel, fiberglass-reinforced plastic, or any reasonably dense, well-damped, sound-reflecting material. For any specific design, there are optimum materials and configurations based on the special requirements of that facility.

VARIABLE ACOUSTICS
One of the unexpected benefits for the school music director who performs in a

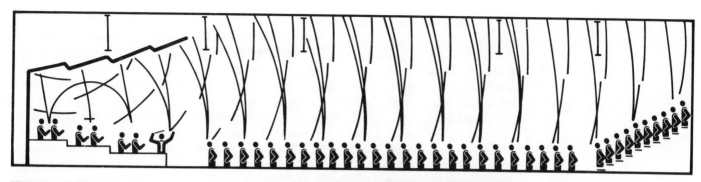

Figure 4. An acoustical shell and canopy. In a proscenium stage auditorium, the audience and performance areas are connected acoustically by the shell or canopy.
Left: Aquinas College, Grand Rapids, Michigan. An outdoor amphitheater adjacent to the music building can provide an excellent location for band concerts and informal music events. Architect: Alfred Liu and Associates. Acoustics: Geerdes Consulting Services.

multipurpose auditorium with adjustable acoustics is the capability for varying the acoustical environment to suit music of different periods or performance by different ensembles. The same movable panels and curtains that are placed in the hall to make it usable for both speech and music can also serve in exciting musical ways if the director is alert to the creative possibilities. Composers such as Bach and Gabrieli, for example, were very much aware of the acoustical ambience in which their music was to be performed, and they probably would have written differently if their halls were different. A number of these halls still are in use—enough to indicate what the acoustics were like for Mozart, Beethoven, and many others. The adjustability built into a school auditorium offers a unique chance, formerly found only in some major concert halls, to perform a composer's music in an acoustical environment similar to that for which it was composed.[7]

The adjustable features designed into a versatile school or college auditorium include some or all of the following:

- A full stage enclosure that incorporates movable forestage side panels and a movable removable ceiling

7. See Harold Geerdes, ''Adjustable Acoustics in Music Performance,'' *Music Educators Journal* 61, no. 8, April 1975, 40–44.

- A portable shell
- Adjustable sound-absorbing treatment on the sides and the rear wall surfaces and sometimes in the ceiling zone of the audience seating area
- Stage curtains of different acoustical qualities
- Moveable ceilings that can close off part of the seating area or change the volume of the hall. This feature was incorporated into the Auditorium Theater in Chicago at the end of the nineteenth century to close off the top balcony, and it has been successfully used in some modern auditoriums as well.

How can adjustable features be used for music performance? A list of some of the optimum acoustical conditions for different types of performances on a scale of dry to reverberant conditions follows:

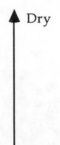

1. Drama, lecture, movies   Dry
2. Band concerts
3. Piano recitals
4. Chamber music
5. Musical theater
6. Opera
7. Orchestra concerts
8. Choir with orchestra
9. Choir alone
10. Organ   Reverberant

A parallel list can be prepared for the music of various composers, ranging from moderately reverberant for Bach and Stravinsky to highly reverberant for Gabrieli. It is relatively simple in an adjustable hall to extend the acoustical control curtains or adjust stage panels to absorb sound and reduce the reverberation time until the desired condition exists.

HEATING AND VENTILATING

The major problem in ventilating an auditorium is moving sufficient air without creating drafts or noise. Since windows are not desirable in an auditorium, all ventilating has to be mechanical. Most ventilating and air conditioning equipment is noisy, and too many auditoriums suffer from a high ambient noise level. Special engineering and installation practices are required, and maximum acceptable levels should be specified for each area, using the numbers of applicable Noise Criterion (NC) curves. NC15 is needed in a 1,000 seat auditorium, and NC25 in a rehearsal room or music classroom, and NC30 or slightly above in a practice room or teaching studio where some masking sound is considered desirable.

Air-conditioning equipment, cooling machinery, and ventilating fans should not be in close proximity to the auditorium. Ducts should contain acoustical lining as well as baffles to prevent the transmission of machinery noises. The amount of air supplied backstage should not cause the front curtain to billow. There must a balance of air between the stage supply and the auditorium supply, and between the stage exhaust and the auditorium exhaust. Drafts in an auditorium, on a stage, or in an orchestra pit can be serious problems. They can affect stage scenery, affect the pitch of instruments, and cause audience discomfort. Keeping the noise level low can be accomplished in part by moving a large of volume of air at low velocity. If grilles are used on the supply ducts, they must not add noise or produce air turbulence. In critical areas, such as practice room suites, the ducts must have reverse path and angles introduced in the duct layout to secure effective sound isolation when adjacent rooms share the same air handling unit. A trained heating and ventilating engineer with auditorium and music room experience (working closely with the acoustical consultant), can meet the requirements for quietness without compromising the comfort of either the performers or the audience.

A good air-conditioning system includes humidity control, which is very important where pianos and wooden or string instruments are stored. Changes in humidity also can affect some of the percussion instruments. Humidity has an effect on acoustics, but just how and to what degree still is being studied. There is no disagreement, however, as to the desirability of year-round constant humidity in music storage, rehearsal, and performance areas.

ILLUMINATION

A well-designed interior environment must have good lighting. Good space relationships and the use of proper materials in the music suite and auditorium can be negated by the wrong choice of lighting systems. Proper lighting of wall surfaces is often neglected when a typical "fixtures and footcandles" approach is used in the lighting design. Lighting of wall surfaces is needed in some spaces for task lighting and in others to enhance the spatial feeling or mood of the room. It makes no sense to spend large amounts of money for beautiful wall materials such as wood paneling, draperies, ceramics, artwork, and so forth, if the surfaces cannot be seen.

Planning the lighting systems to provide the necessary task lighting while maintaining the proper ambient light level in the space is very important for comfortable viewing and attractive surroundings. The Illuminating Engineering Society (IES) recommends that the ambient light level be approximately one-third of the task lighting. While so-called "Task/Ambient" lighting systems are not appropriate for all spaces, they should be considered where the task lighting levels are high.

Good results are seldom achieved if the lighting design is added after the entire architectural concept has been developed. Lighting must be considered carefully as one of the basic design elements. Therefore, architects should have the input of a competent lighting consultant (if they do not have in-house expertise) early in the planning and design stage. Satisfactory lighting for music departments cannot be realized without an understanding of the visual problems encountered and the architect should be aware of them.

Some of these considerations are:

- In music rooms, small details are important. Lack of uniformity in manuscript, ink, and paper, as well as inconsistent size of music symbols and printing methods add to the difficulty.
- The instrument played and the necessity of sharing music often results in awkward positioning of the music at an unusual distance from the eyes. Visual comfort and efficiency sometimes are sacrificed for appearance in adjusting music racks.
- Musicians are expected to read rapidly and accurately while also following the conductor's motions.
- Irregular seating arrangements force musicians to face the director from various angles and complicate the problems of glare and distracting objects entering the visual field.
- Music rooms necessarily are equipped with furnishings that can create a condition of visual clutter.
- When platforms are used, musicians standing or sitting on the top levels have a different relationship with light sources located in the ceiling than do those people sitting at floor level or standing on the director's podium.
- The angle of lighting is critical in performance situations because performers must look up at the conductor as well as view their music. This places certain strictures on the use of front lighting in an acoustical shell or on a stage.
- Music rooms are used day and night, summer and winter, for varied activities, some of which are nonmusical and thus have many different lighting requirements.

In addition to the visual problems, the lighting systems in any space devoted to music teaching, rehearsing, or performing must comply with rigid noise requirements.

Quality versus quantity

Whether in a standard classroom or a music classroom, comfortable, functional lighting depends as much on the quality of the lighting installations as the quantity of light provided. The level of illumination must be sufficient in footcandles, but even more important is the elimination of direct and reflected glare (veiling reflections), high contrast, and shadows. Attention should be paid to the following factors:

- Providing proper illumination levels on visual tasks (footcandles). See IES recommendations.
- Keeping brightness of light sources and surfaces within acceptable levels (footlamberts).
- Controlling contrast and brightness ratios (a) between light sources and ceiling, (b) between the printed page and the floor or walls, (c) between windows and walls, and (d) between music background and conductor backgrounds.
- Providing proper diffusion of light to eliminate objectionable reflections, shadows, and bright spots.
- Other considerations such as those described below.

Illumination levels for school tasks have been the subject of continuing research, as shown in publications such as *American Standard Practice for School Lighting* and the Illuminating Engineering Society's *Lighting Handbook*. A minimum of thirty footcandles for reading simple scores and seventy footcandles for complex scores is compatible with IES published standards. This would indicate that no less that seventy footcandles be provided by general illumination in the rehearsal room or on stage. If proper diffusion and good angles can exist, this should be adequate for the performance. Some carefully placed front lighting helps to soften shadows and improve the visual image for the audience. Flexibility in lighting levels and separate area controls enhance the enjoyment of audiences attending recitals, concerts, lectures, or films, and is essential for drama, musical theater, and similar productions.

Whatever types of light sources or lighting fixtures are selected, brightness can be controlled by careful selection of diffusers, fixture housings, louvers, and lenses as

Type of lighting	Function	Controlled from	Fixtures/Instruments
House	Light audience area	Lighting control board	Incandescent only
Stage	Light performance area	Lighting control board	Floodlights, spotlights, scoops, special lights
Concert	Light performance area	Lighting control board	Downlights, floodlights
Work	Light rehearsal area with stage lights off	Wall switches, stage manager's control panel, lighting control board	General
Rehearsal	Light rehearsal area with stage lights off	Stage manager's control panel, lighting control board	Downlights, general lighting
Emergency	Permit audience and performers to escape if building power fails	Automatic switchover from house and stage circuits	May use some house lighting fixtures or separate floodlights
Panic	Provide immediate full light in the event of a panic in which building power does not fail	Stage manager's control panel, lighting control board	Uses existing systems
Aisle and exit	Light steps and aisle and pinpoint doors to provide safe egress from audience area when house is darkened	Lighting control board, panelboard	Special

Figure 5. Lighting requirements for a music/drama auditorium

well as proper sizes of lamps and the positioning of fixtures. For instance, low-brightness parabolic diffusers can be used on fluorescent fixtures, thus preventing the ceiling from being the brightest surface in the room. Whatever the source, consideration should be given to the noise level and its dimming capability as well as to the proper selection of materials. In every installation, the designer must take into account first costs, ease of maintenance, repair and replacement, size, appearance, color, and heating effect. Contrast and brightness ratios must be controlled to add visual comfort and efficiency. The brightness ratio between the music rack surfaces and the music should be limited to 3:1. This suggests lightly colored nonglare finishes on the face of the rack. The music stand is usually in the field of vision of other players and should be finished to blend with the surroundings. The appearance of the stands and folios to the audience when the group appears in concert also should be considered. Woodwork and furnishings for the music rooms should meet the recommended reflectance range. The floor should not be too dark. Green chalkboards easily are held in line with the recommended brightness ratio of the board to its wall background. Boards with higher than 20 percent reflectance reduce the contrast of chalk with board, and the visibility of chalk marks suffers accordingly. Steel chalkboards with fired abrasive enamel surfaces enable magnets to be used.

Proper diffusion of light is a function of the type of shielding or materials used as diffusers on the fixtures themselves; the number and distribution on the fixtures themselves; the number and distributions of fixtures; and the selection of light-colored, matte-finished materials for walls, furnishings, and equipment that will reflect light without glare. This will help control reflected brightness, which is as much a problem as direct brightness.[8] Proper diffusion of light also depends upon the selection of light-colored matte-finished materials for walls, ceilings, furnishings, and equipment. This will help control reflected brightness that is as much a problem as direct brightness from the light sources.

Other important considerations are first costs, operating costs, lamp life and ease of maintenance, repair and replacement, color appearance, heating effect, noise levels and dimming capabilities as well as lighting control systems.

Natural versus artificial

With increased awareness of energy conservation, daylight has been "rediscovered" as a light source. Unilateral daylight from windows at one side of the room is commonly used. While popular and practical, it does involve a number of inherent problems:

- Natural light is not dependable.
- Sunlight is not available for evening and night rehearsals.
- Students near the windows may have very high levels of light (100 footcandles or more), with levels falling off rapidly to the inside rows where there may be less than five footcandles on a bright day. Sky glare also can be a problem.
- Windows that serve some students well as a source of light can be a source of glare and discomfort to the director or others in the room.
- At night, windows usually become dark areas. Proper shades are usually able to solve the problems of both glare and dark areas. Direct sunlight on windows is typically controlled by closing blinds or shades, thereby preventing the use of available natural light. Control of direct sunlight is made relatively easy by using such devices as reflective blinds or light shelves that reflect light to the ceiling that diffuses the light and reflects it into the space. Depending upon building orienta-

---

8. Reflectance values of different color samples may be seen inside the back cover of the IES *Lighting Handbook* (5th Edition).

tion, direct sunlight can also be controlled by the use of exterior shading from roof overhangs, horizontal shutters, and trees. Sunlight can also be used effectively by means of properly designed light scoops, clerestories, and roof monitors that diffuse the light before it is introduced into the space. Although the use of daylight can enhance the space and affect some economies in the operating cost of the lighting system, the overall effect of the heating and cooling systems must also be considered. It is possible that the use of sunlight for its supplemental lighting and solar heating capabilities can effect substantial energy savings and at the same time provide the bonus of more agreeable spaces for the various activities.

In many school designs, music rooms as well as lecture rooms and auditoriums have been built without windows. This can simplify the design of the lighting system. In addition to lighting considerations, there are other good arguments for a windowless room, such as easier control of the acoustical and thermal environment, easier adaptability for use of visual aids, and elimination of distractions. Proper uses of lighting, different building materials, and color can eliminate the claustrophobic atmosphere of such rooms.

MAINTENANCE AND LIGHT CONTROL

Particular attention should be paid to maintenance of the lighting system. Without a planned program of fixture cleaning and replacement of lamps, illumination levels can drop to one-half of the installed values. In auditoriums or other high-ceilinged rooms where scaffolding is required to replace lamps, it is more efficient to replace all the lamps at one time. Lamp life can be predicted accurately and a relamping and cleaning program can be scheduled at intervals that approach the useful life of the lamps.

Care always should be taken to relamp fluorescent fixtures with the proper color of lamps. Illumination levels as well as the colors of walls are greatly affected by the choice of fluorescent lamp color. The lumen output per watt of electricity (efficacy) is highest with cool white and warm white lamps, and thus is the primary reason these sources are used. However, recent developments in lamp design have produced lamps that have better color rendition properties but lower efficiencies. The deluxe cool white lamp has the best color rendering (that is, nearest to natural daylight) and complements the colors of furnishings, clothing, and healthy skin tones. Deluxe warm white lamps can be used where a much warmer atmosphere and good color rendering is desired, and they are compatible with incandescent lighting. Other recently developed fluorescent lamps have combined higher efficiencies with better color rendering and should be considered when designing a new system or retrofitting an existing system.

Although the most commonly used light sources are incandescent and fluorescent (due to their lower initial cost), other sources have been developed that have some advantages. For example, the metal halide lamp shares the advantage of long life with the fluorescents, has higher efficiency, and excellent color rendering capabilities. It is also a smaller, more compact light source than fluorescent lights and can be used in fixtures similar to those using incandescent bulbs.

When using fixtures with fluorescent or metal halide lamps, attention should be given to noise control, especially if dimming the lights in the fixtures is to be considered. Unlike incandescent fixtures, these fixtures contain ballasts for starting and operating the lamps. Low-noise ballasts should always be specified for music facilities. The lights in these fixtures can be dimmed at extra expense by substituting dimming ballasts. It may be appropriate to place ballasts and dimming equipment in a remote location to eliminate possible noise problems. A more economical method of creating varying light levels can be used by using selective switching to combine easily dimmable incandescent fixtures with the other types of lighting.

Two separate lighting systems are used in this auditorium: dimmable incandescent lamps for performances and fluorescent lights for classroom use.

AUDIENCE AREAS

Lighting levels in the auditorium seating area need not be high unless the room is also used as a classroom. For reading performance programs, twenty footcandles is sufficient, but the system should be dimmable. For classroom use, at least thirty footcandles is needed. The source for classroom lighting can be a completely separate fixture system, with its own separate controls. For public performances, however, flexible control of the house lighting is important, and a number of separate dimmable circuits should be used to provide light in different areas and at varying quantities. Aisle and exit lights must not interfere with stage lighting effects. Emergency egress lighting must also be incorporated into the lighting design, providing fixtures powered by an emergency power source that turns on automatically in case of a power failure.

AUDITORIUM LIGHTING

Lighting the stage for performances can be as simple or as sophisticated as finances permit. A review of the projected uses for the auditorium produces a parallel list of lighting requirements for both the performing and audience areas, and must include the legal requirements for public safety. A complete lighting package that meets the needs of both dramatic and musical productions must be designed to meet the particular situation, since programming of activities and architectural considerations differ. Lighting engineers can work as consultants to advise the architect's lighting designers of the design specifications. Figure 5 provides a checklist of features that are included in a complete lighting system for a music/drama auditorium. Such a system requires the following components:

- House lighting (some tied to emergency lighting, all tied to the panic lighting system)
- Battery-powered emergency lighting (if separate from above)
- Aisle lighting
- Exit lighting
- Portable stage lighting
- Backstage performance lighting (running lights)
- General backstage lighting (some tied to emergency, all tied to panic)
- Rehearsal lighting
- Load circuit plugging boxes
- Load circuit plugging strips
- Load circuit floor pockets
- Interconnecting panel (can be omitted if a control circuit is provided for each load circuit)
- Stage house lighting control console
- Preset panel (if appropriate)
- Memory bank (if appropriate)
- Dimmer bank

Optional features to be considered if the auditorium is to be used by road shows are: a company switch, which enables traveling groups to wire their control board and operate lights through their own system; a Front of House (FOH) transfer panel which allows auditorium circuits for front of house lighting to be plugged into the traveling control system; and remote stage and house lighting control stations, appropriately placed to enable one person to carry out all lighting control functions for films, simple concerts, and other auditorium activities.

COLOR

The selection of proper colors for all areas is an important detail in planning that often is neglected. This is an element that costs little extra money and that often can save money in future maintenance if done carefully. Color selection is particularly important in the music department because of the subtle interplay between psychological and musical factors, especially in the rehearsal and performance of bands, orchestras, and choirs. The public also is sensitive to the effects of color on the performing/listening environment.

School auditoriums can be attractive without costly decorative features. Intelligent choice of materials and colors can do much to enhance the overall visual impression. Such a simple idea as varying the color of upholstery from seat to seat adds visual interest that is eye-catching and yet adds little to the cost. Whether selected by an interior designer, a color consultant, a school committee (hopefully not), or the architect, color should be based on the following considerations:

- Color affects and influences people of all ages. Tests have shown that some colors stimulate and excite while other create fatigue, depression, and irritation.
- Color plays an important role in creating an atmosphere that promotes efficiency and morale.
- Selecting colors that are merely attractive may force those who occupy schoolrooms to work and study in surroundings that are psychologically unsuitable. For example, abnormally high color contrasts have adverse effects. Such surroundings gradually may become irritating, affect work, and cause distress and unhappiness. Elimination of adverse conditions not only stimulates energy and improves concentration, but also raises morale. Color can help to bring about a better spirit of cooperation among teachers and students.
- The correct use of color, combined with proper maintenance, gives teachers and students a feeling of pride in their surroundings and fosters a desire to keep them neat and orderly.

Warm and cool

The blues and greens associated with the sky, lakes, and trees are cool colors. They frequently are recommended for rooms with western and southern exposures, which may feel overly warm from the sunshine. On the other hand, pale shades of yellow, orange, pink, and tan are warm colors. They frequently are recommended for classrooms with northern and eastern exposures. Cool, light pastels are receding colors that tend to make a room seem larger. The reverse generally is true of the warm colors. Greens, especially blue-greens, are quiet colors to which few people object.

Determining values

Color value in schoolrooms is important in two ways: Lighter values should be used in rooms that tend to be dark, thus ensuring the maximum light reflection. More brightly lit rooms may have darker walls. In rooms receiving strong glaring light, colors of medium or darker value reduce the strength of the reflected light. Color values can be used to equalize the distribution of reflected daylight in a room. Light and dark color values can be used to change the apparent proportions of a long narrow room by painting the end walls in a relatively dark color and using a lighter value of that color or a harmonizing hue on the long side walls. When juxtaposed, dark colors seem to advance and light colors appear to retreat, making the length appear to diminish and the width increase. In square or nearly square rooms, the uninteresting proportion can be made less apparent by painting one wall a hue different from that of the other three. The concentration of interest on one wall makes the sameness of dimension less noticeable. If a window wall is used for this purpose, it should be lighter than the others. If an opposite wall is used, it should be darker than the other three, in accordance with the rules of equalizing light.

Placement

Monotony throughout a school can be avoided by the choice and placement of colors. In classrooms, where it is important to secure and retain the attention of the students, color can help by providing a focal wall. The focal wall usually is a darker value of the color used on the other three walls, or a contrasting color that focuses attention on that part of the room. However, the color must not cause eyestrain. A slightly darker value usually is more restful than lighter colors.

The atmosphere in which teachers work should be an important consideration. They never should be forced to look into strong light. Wherever possible, the teacher should face a wall painted in a restful color. If a focal color is used on the front wall, the same color should be used on the opposite wall if the teacher faces it often. Because the light in a classroom usually comes from only one direction, it seems particularly strong and concentrated on the wall opposite the window. The reflected light often is equalized by the use of wall colors in three values. The darkest color is applied to the wall opposite the windows where the light is strongest. The two end walls, which receive slightly less direct light, are painted in a lighter value, and the window wall, which receives little or no direct light, is painted the lightest value.

In an average classroom, the ceiling should reflect the maximum amount of light. This restricts the color range to white, off-white, or a very pale tint of the wall color or a contrasting tint. Such colors should have reflection factors within the range of 80 to 85 percent.[9] Where the maximum amount of light need not be reflected from the ceiling, a more pronounced color is not only effective from a decorative standpoint, but also serves a functional purpose. In a room with a cold northern or eastern exposure, a ceiling in sunny yellow or light orange gives a cheerful effect. The glare of light from the west or south can be countered effectively by using light green or blue-green on the ceiling.

---

9. IES *Lighting Handbook*, back cover.

Selection

Room volume and shape, carpets, draperies, seats, wall treatments, stage floor, light spill from projectors or other theater lighting instruments, and stage drapes used for masking or scenery are all variables that must be taken into consideration when selecting colors for the auditorium. Areas that are to be invisible to the audience, such as the roof deck or upper side walls adjacent to a catwalk, must be flat black. Aside from these requirements, a small auditorium may use cool receding colors for vertical areas with the ceiling a contrasting warm hue. Larger auditoriums may use warm colors or a variety of warm and cool colors.

A music room may be treated as an area of some stimulation, employing warm and cool colors. Consideration should be given to the color of walls adjoining chalkboards, the color of the boards themselves, and the walls behind the conductor, all of which might be sources of eyestrain if too much contrast is present.

Offices should use both natural and artificial light for maximum eye comfort. Where the light is of higher intensity than required, colors having lower light reflection factors should be used. Where the light is adequate or slightly low, the color should have a higher light reflection factor. Where indirect lighting is used, the ceiling should be white.

Rooms where students occasionally are assembled should have an atmosphere as different as possible from their classrooms. The color background not only should be restful and relaxing, but also should put the student in the proper mental attitude to participate wholeheartedly in the activities of the assembly.

Relationship to the lighting system

An important factor in the selection of colors is the original and *maintained* relationship with the lighting system. Lamps come in a wide variety of colors from incandescent warm tones to the various whites of fluorescent and metal halide lamps. The most commonly used have been the incandescent and cool white fluorescent lamps. However, the improved color rendering properties of other sources, plus the increased availability of new fixture designs have increased the use of a wide variety of light sources. The original intention of a color scheme in a room can be lost completely by changing types of lamps in the lighting system. Colored lights affect colored paints in ways that often are unpredictable. Many times a room is repainted without regard to physical or psychological needs simply because there is leftover paint of a particular color or because a color can be obtained inexpensively. However, it is important to keep a coordinated maintenance program of lighting and decorating that recognizes the two are interdependent.

ELECTRICAL INSTALLATIONS

Many of the electrical considerations have been discussed in chapter three and in earlier parts of this chapter. Additionally, the installation of conduit for both audio and video cable should be included in the regular electrical contract. Since extra conduit is relatively inexpensive if installed during building construction, it makes good sense to provide extra conduit to each music room, all of which is connected to a central recording or control room. If such a room is not available, conduit can be connected to a space adjacent to the school office. From there, closed-circuit or regular radio or television equipment may be installed and fed into a distribution system through this conduit. If fluorescent lights are specified, they must have Type A quiet ballasts that will not interfere with music teaching or rehearsing. Areas where recording is done should be lighted with incandescent fixtures that will not cause a noise problem. Electrical installations in listening laboratories and electronic piano labs should be safeguarded, with all electrical connections concealed and protected. A record should be kept of where concealed conduit runs. Access for servicing should be made as easy as possible.

Left: Computerized lighting control consoles are compact and flexible.
Below: Pioneer Auditorium, East Grand Rapids, Michigan. The audio control console should be out in the audience area where the operator can hear the reinforced sound directly. Space for scripts or for tape recorders should be provided. Sound system: Ascom.

AUDITORIUM AUDIO SYSTEMS

Sound reinforcement

Most auditoriums of more than 200–300 seats have sound systems. A good system, properly operated, is set at the lowest acceptable level and does not blare. In fact, the best sound amplification is undetectable. To accomplish this, the entire system must be of professional quality. If directionality of sound is to be retained, loudspeakers must be placed above the performing area—never at the two sides. Portable or temporary systems seldom are satisfactory.

Because of the increasing use of amplified instruments, adequate line inputs on stage or sub-master mixer should be included.

The entire system should have the frequency response and fidelity of the best available home systems. Stereo systems will be appropriate in certain situations. Today's sophisticated listeners can hardly be expected to leave their compact disc/ultra-high fidelity system at home to attend auditorium functions reproduced through a tinny system with poor fidelity.

A point-source system is one with a single central loudspeaker cluster and generally is recommended. Loudspeakers in the ceiling may be used when the auditorium ceiling is too low or sight lines are too poor to properly accommodate a central system. Ceiling speaker systems, sometimes called distributed systems, often are inadequate because of the following:

- The frequency response of the loudspeaker and its associated line-matching transformer are inadequate and thus unable to reproduce natural, full-range sound.
- The typical small metal back-box restricts the low frequency response, and the usual baffle prevents smooth, even distribution of frequencies above 5,000 Hz.
- Insufficient loudspeakers are provided for proper distribution. A realistic coverage angle for an eight-inch loudspeaker is 60°, and it is considered good practice to provide 50 percent overlap at the listener's ear. A room with a ceiling of eight to ten feet or more would require a large number of speakers.
- Insufficient power is one of the most common failures in a distributed speaker system. It leads to distortion that includes loudspeaker overload as well as amplifier overload. This can be avoided by providing both an amplifier and a speaker system that are used conservatively at one-tenth their rated capability.

If these shortcomings are avoided carefully, a distributed speaker system can be effective. Additional precautions should be taken in large auditoriums with a long distance between the stage and rear seats. Ceiling loudspeakers there may require a time-delay unit so that loudspeaker sound will not reach listeners in the back row before it arrives from the live source in the front of the room. Figure 6 shows the sound system requirements for multipurpose auditoriums.

If the auditorium is to be used for traveling road shows, provisions should be made for plugging the visitor's equipment into the house system.

In the usual system of bidding and awarding contracts for school buildings, the sound system frequently is listed as a part of the electrical contract, with the winning electrical firm subcontracting the system in turn to the lowest bidder. Since school contracts seldom include performance specifications for the sound system, this is one place where the contractor can cut corners. To guarantee a good sound reinforcement system, it should be designed by a competent sound engineer. The engineer must get adequate information from the future user and then draw up specifications that will include equipment by brand name and number. If at all possible, the sound system should be separate from the electrical contract, and should be an independent agreement between the school and the sound system contractor. The work should be reviewed and tested by the sound engineer to be certain it meets specifications before it is accepted.

The control position for an auditorium sound system must be placed within the

System function	Required for
Figure 6. Sound system requirements for a music/drama auditorium	
Sound reinforcement	Audience listening
Program monitors	Control rooms, warm-up and dressing room, box office, lobby areas
Fold-back	Onstage performers of rock and amplified music
Recording	Later listening by performers; possible radio or record use
Sound effects	Dramatic productions
Playback	Playing the records or tapes into the audience chamber
Audience recall and paging	Signalling end of intermission (may be played through program monitors if no separate bell system is used)

audience chamber where the operator hears the direct sound as the audience hears it. Locating it in a control room where the signal is processed through mixers, amplifiers, and speakers is too unreliable for effective and subtle sound control. Microphones must be placed near the source of sounds and must be arranged carefully to give good balance if more than one source is amplified. For operatic and theater performances, a number of microphones can be placed in the footlights with proper resilient mounting to avoid thumping sounds from walking on stage. The operator in the control booth must follow the performance and enable only those microphones that are near the sources to be amplified. For orchestral or choir amplification, additional microphones are needed overhead and the relative operating levels must be monitored and adjusted. Many musicians are prejudiced against amplification. However, high-quality, professional-grade equipment, operated skillfully, can enhance the quality of many musical performances. This is especially true in large convention halls or gymnasiums, and outdoors where the background sound level is intrusive. The design of each sound system should not be left to suppliers of equipment.

Recording and broadcasting

Improvements in recording equipment and televised education have led schools to incorporate facilities for these techniques. Space should be allowed for both receiving and broadcasting music. The control booth should be well insulated and should have slanted double glass windows for viewing the performing groups. Such a control booth can be located either adjacent to the auditorium stage or between rehearsal halls. The ideal location, however, is at the rear of the auditorium adjacent to lighting control, sound effects, sound reinforcement, and other systems. Integration or at least juxtaposition of these control areas makes possible more efficient operation, which is particularly important when several systems are used simultaneously, such as for music theater or operettas.

The control booth is the electronic nerve center of the building, and conduit for audio and video cables should connect it to every music classroom, rehearsal room, and teaching studio, as well as to various locations in the auditorium. Easy access to the rooftop for antenna connections and to the basement for cable runs in open troughs (which are much less expensive than conduit and just as good for audio/video

Right: Eastchester High School auditorium, Eastchester, New York. The booth for recording and broadcasting, videotaping, and lighting control should be equipped with operable windows and a house intercom system. Architect: David Paul Helpern, P.C. Photograph by Wolfgang Hoyt Esto.

Below: Towsley Center School of Music, University of Michigan, Ann Arbor. The sound control booth should be located at the rear of the auditorium, adjacent to the lighting control booth. Architect: TMP Associates. Acoustics: R. Lawrence Kirkegaard and Associates. Photograph by Balthazar Korab.

cables) also should be provided. The size and layout of the recording sound-control booth often is compromised in order to gain a desirable location. Such accommodation to space, however, should not penalize present or future programs. The assistance of a trained sound engineer will help produce the best room design for efficient use. The equipment to be installed will have an effect on room layout and size.

Music playback

Provision for music playback in the auditorium, rehearsal rooms, music classrooms, and perhaps other rooms should be included in the planning stage. Such matters as placement of wall-mounted loudspeakers, for example, need to be determined so that concealed conduit for speaker cables can be installed. Electrical outlets must be strategically placed. In many cases, the local playback system can be fed from the recording booth. Equipment for music playback must be compatible with the primary systems in the control booth. It must be of good quality, high fidelity, and preferably designed into the space where it is to be used—not added after the fact. It should be versatile and accommodate various modes.

Electronic music

Complete music facilities often include a specially equipped studio for the composition of electronic music. Low-cost equipment for this purpose is increasingly available. Many universities have electronic music studios staffed by professionals who can advise on the type of space and equipment required. Equipment may include synthesizers, tone generators, tape recorders (preferably with variable speed control), filters, mixers, amplifiers, reverberation devices, time-delay units, duplicating facilities, and monitor loudspeakers. Adequate shelving to house the equipment, concealed conduit or cable troughs, and a convenient workbench and tape-editing facility should be provided, as well as ample storage space for tapes and records.

House intracommunication

Every auditorium should be provided with equipment for house intracommunication. The number of stations and their locations will depend on the programming plans for the facility, but a useful checklist of positions to be considered is the following:
- Light control booth
- Sound effects position
- Recording booth
- Projection location
- Stage left
- Stage right
- Conductor's position, orchestra lift
- Lighting catwalks
- Manager's office
- Box office
- Dressing rooms
- Drama director's position: row ten or eleven in the auditorium (a removable phone plugs into a floor outlet)
- Drama director's position: rear-auditorium control booth

For more elaborate productions, a stage manager's desk and panel with provision for communicating with performers and other technicians is very useful; it is nearly indispensable for Broadway-type shows. The auditorium communication system can be tied into the central school system if desired. In this case, special precautions must be taken to prevent feeding announcements or broadcasts into the auditorium during public performances.

Sound effects

The music director rarely has occasion to call upon a sound effects system. But a drama coach sharing an auditorium with the music department would find it hard to accept a hall without one. In its simplest form, it should be able to play tapes through an amplifier and have a switching system that will feed audio signals to a number of locations at the sides, rear, or above the stage. These lines terminate in audio receptacles that can accept plugs for portable loudspeakers.

AUDITORIUM VISUAL SYSTEMS

Scenery projection

Open stages and modified proscenium stages frequently use projected backgrounds. When delivered from a catwalk or ceiling slot above the stage, optical correction makes possible a rather steep angle that permits actors to come within five feet of the image without blocking the light path. Best results are obtained when the screen is permanent—preferably plaster on a wall—and thus not subject to unevenness or to movement from drafts on stage (both of which will distort the image and destroy its effectiveness). The screen should not be beaded to avoid reflecting stage lighting to the audience. Rear projection is another system that can be used for scenery and other theatrical effects. It is especially effective for television, and requires space behind a translucent screen rather than an opaque one.

Slides and movies

State and local fire codes restrict the kinds of movie projectors that can be used in an open auditorium or in a projection room that is not enclosed completely and equipped with a sprinkler system. The 16mm movie projectors meet these requirements and can be equipped with long-throw lenses to make projection from a rear booth practical. Since movie machines are noisy, they should be confined to an isolated booth. When this is not possible, portable enclosures can be devised for in-house movie projection. In either case, provision must be made for connecting into the house sound system, with a remote volume control at the operator's position. If movies are projected from a booth, a monitor loudspeaker must be provided and equipped with its own volume control. A remote house-lighting dimmer within easy reach of the projectionist will facilitate one-person operation of house lighting, movie sound, and picture.

Slide projectors that throw a bright picture from the rear of an auditorium are very costly, so slides usually must be shown from a closer position. The noise of the fan can be very distracting when it is placed within range of the audience. Provision for remote operation will allow a lecturer to advance the slides from the stage. Proper placement of the projection screen is a consideration if it is to be permanently mounted. It must be at the proper height to avoid distortion of the projected image and must not interfere with stage lighting or other accoutrements.

Television

The development of public television for educational purposes and the perfection of video recording (especially the videocassette recorder and closed-circuit television systems) make planning for use of these tools important. This can be integrated into plans for audio recording and radio reception. The decision to incorporate television in a school probably will not be made to fulfill the needs of the music department alone. Nevertheless, there are certain uses of this teaching tool that music educators should consider in planning for the future. Closed circuit television is used increasingly to provide general education experiences in music for the whole student body. Conduits from the stage and sound control room to selected positions throughout the school will enable such use. If a complete system is considered too costly at inception, the conduit should be installed in the building at the time of construction when its cost is relatively low. The auditorium also should be equipped for large group viewing with video projection systems provided. Television monitoring systems may be helpful in some practice rooms. Informal instrumental instruction sometimes is presented on educational television and schools may want to provide the means of receiving these lessons in the music department. The portable videocassette recorder is a tool of great potential value to music educators. The video disc is another recent development that may offer possibilities to music education.

Special effects

Special effects can be either visual or aural. Black lights or strobe lights use floor outlets in the front of the stage controlled from the lighting booth. "Full surround" sound or rotating sound easily are possible if conduit to six or eight loudspeaker positions is located around the perimeter of the audience seating area.

CHAPTER 5

HOW TO MAKE THE MOST OF EXISTING FACILITIES

Most music educators will not have the opportunity to teach in new or upgraded facilities, so it is important that they know how to make the most of what they have. This chapter lists problems commonly found in classrooms, auditoriums, and other music rooms and some available remedies. Music teachers often complain about their facilities. The following material will give them concrete ideas of what to do about them so they meet their needs more adequately.

CLASSROOMS

Classrooms in which music history, appreciation, or theory are taught should meet the following criteria:

- The room acoustics should be appropriate for music and should be designed with adequate reverberation to make singing and listening clear and pleasant.
- The ceiling should not be covered entirely with acoustical tile. Placing all absorption on a single plane is not an effective way of treating any space, classroom, rehearsal room, or performance space.
- All electrical and mechanical systems should be very quiet to avoid covering soft music passages. The heating/ventilating system should not exceed a noise criterion of NC25, which under-window unit ventilators never achieve. Noise criterion graphs are available in mechanical engineering handbooks and the room noise levels can be measured with a sound level meter. Fluorescent lighting fixtures should not be used because they produce an objectionable sixty-cycle hum that renders them inappropriate for music rooms.

COMMON CLASSROOM PROBLEMS AND SOLUTIONS

Problems	Solutions
Excessive ceiling acoustical tile; "dry" conditions; poor acoustics	Seal all or part of the ceiling tile with paint to reduce absorption or replace some tile with drop-in hardboard. The middle two-thirds can be reflective, with an absorptive four- to six-foot band around the periphery of the ceiling, and also the top two or three feet of the side walls.
Noisy ventilators that exceed NC25 acceptable noise criterion level	Adjust the pulleys on ventilators to slow noisy fans and reduce interference. (This will reduce ventilating capacity somewhat, but the reduced noise level will be of greater value.)

| Noisy lighting fixtures, often with an annoying pitch level | Replace ballasts in fluorescent lighting fixtures with quieter Type A ballasts. Or move ballasts to a remote location, pehaps to a closet or other noncritical space. |

STUDIOS AND PRACTICE ROOMS

These rooms should have good acoustical separation from adjoining spaces. Each room should have the following characteristics:

- Doors should be solid core.
- Doors should have sound-seal stripping around sides and top and a drop-seal at the threshold. To test if the doors are properly sealed, insert a piece of typing paper between the seal and the door frame, then close the door. It should hold the paper and keep it from being removed (air tight is sound tight). The drop-seal at the floor has a screw that easily adjust the closure, and the side seals should also be adjustable. Install a drop-seal if one does not exist. The seals should be checked and adjusted once or twice a year to compensate for compression and wear.
- Rooms should be equipped with lined air ducts to reduce noise. Introducing right angles in the duct runs also helps reduce "crosstalk" between rooms.
- To improve the level of sound containment, add one or two layers of gypsum board on walls. Mount the board using resilient clips on the furring strips. This is to deaden sound between rooms. Overlap the joints and use two different thicknesses of wallboard if possible. Caulk all joints (floor, ceiling, and side walls) with special nonhardening acoustical sealant. Be sure any wall penetrations such as pipes and electrical outlets are all sealed with fiberglass and caulked to be made airtight. A sound absorptive blanket between the furring strips will also help.
- To deaden sound within rooms, apply sound absorption to at least two adjoining walls. These should be impact-resistant acoustical panels or constructed of special materials suitable for this application. Carpeting on the floors will also help quiet the room.

REHEARSAL ROOMS

- A good rehearsal room will have sufficient room area and volume to accommodate the largest ensemble.

A good rehearsal room has a flat floor for maximum flexibility, operable draperies for acoustical adjustability, and convenient in-room storage for large bulky instruments.

Shelby High School, Shelby, Michigan. A band rehearsal room that is too live can be vastly improved by the addition of homemade special absorptive panels that can also add color to the room. Any wall material should be resistant to impact by instruments. Acoustics: Geerdes Consulting Services. Photograph by Jory Holmes.

- The room acoustics should be neither too live nor too dead. Controlled, balanced sound and tonal clarity are essential elements of good rehearsal room acoustics that can be achieved only with good room volume, proper room shape, and carefully designed interior finishes on ceilings and walls. Also, placing acoustical tile only on the ceiling is not an adequate way to make a rehearsal room a good teaching area. Reverberation time is only one of the important aspects of rehearsal room acoustics.
- Adjustability of both acoustical and physical elements is desirable, particularly if the rehearsal room is to be shared by any combination of band, orchestra, or chorus. This may mean using movable acoustical draperies or wall panels and portable risers.
- Quiet and adequate lighting and ventilating systems are very important and difficult to achieve without special effort. Fluorescent lighting fixtures should have remote ballasts or Type A quiet ballasts. Metal halide lamps are not suitable in rehearsal rooms because of their noise and their delayed response when turned on.
- A rehearsal room should be sealed well enough to inhibit external sounds intruding from either inside or outside the building, and rehearsal sounds should be confined to the rooms so they do not detract from activities in adjoining spaces.
- To facilitate rehearsals, room should have proper posture seats, convenient storage for instruments, robes, uniforms, and other equipment, and good traffic flow in and out of storage and rehearsal spaces. (Analyze the facilities carefully with an eye to improving equipment, making storage more suitable, and rerouting student traffic.)

To improve rehearsal room acoustics:
- Treat the walls with acoustical panels that absorb or reflect sound as required. Multiuse rooms with fixed acoustics should add retractable acoustical draperies.
- Add additional absorption if the the room is too live. This can be in the form of sound absorbing panels or heavy velour draperies weighing sixteen ounces or more per square yard, have at least 150 percent fullness, and are lined with felt (if maximum absorption is needed). Also, the curtains should be hung no less than eight to ten inches from the wall. Dividing large draped areas into sections will

increase their flexibility. For example, two twenty-foot panels are better than one forty-foot panel.

- If the sound is uneven in the room, dispersion can be added in the form of splays on the front walls above doors and chalkboards using steel studs and gypsum board, splaying one foot or more in each four feet. The addition of diffuser panels also can help spread the sound evenly throughout the room and improve the ability of players to hear across the ensemble.
- As a last choice, adding carpet to the rehearsal room floor can lower sound levels when other options do not seem practicable or do not produce the desired results. Music groups seldom perform on carpeted floors.

PERFORMANCE AREAS

While the real teaching process is carried on primarily in classrooms and rehearsal rooms, the performance areas are probably the most important, because it is here where the music department meets the public: the parents, the school board, and the taxpayers who support the school and the music program.

Auditorium

For a thorough discussion of design considerations, the audience-to-stage relationship and the advantages of the one-room "open stage," see page 45. The subject of acoustics is discussed on pages 64–72.

Common problems in existing auditoriums are:
- An acoustically dead proscenium "picture frame" stage with a flyloft above and heavy stage curtains around it.
- Poor sight/sound lines.

Sound absorbent panels on at least two adjoining walls of the practice room will improve room acoustics.

- Inadequate volume for good sound mix and reverberation.
- Noisy ventilation systems.

The problem auditorium can be improved for musical performances:

- A proscenium stage should have a reflective ceiling suspended over it to improve onstage communication, project sound energy out to the audience area, and make the auditorium as much as "one-room" space as possible. A hard-surfaced stage shell should surround the performers. These are best purchased from firms that specialize in performing arts equipment. Shells made on-site are too heavy, unwieldy, inflexible, and not worth the coast savings that might be expected.
- Stage risers help project sound and also improve sightlines for proud parents as well as performers.
- Gypsum board or plaster pockets are recommended to enclose retracted absorbing stage curtains so that during musical performances the curtains are out of the sound field.
- Quieting noisy ventilating systems that mask soft musical passages is very difficult and often costly. An architect can usually recommend a mechanical engineer who has had some successful experience in this field. The principles involved are: isolating violation from the building structure; lining air ducts with fiberglass; using quiet terminal devices that do not add turbulence; and moving a lot of air slowly.
- Renovation of old auditoriums can successfully include acoustical upgrading, which in itself is a valid reason for renovation that should not be overlooked.

Cafetorium

These are very seldom even moderately successful and the combination of a cafeteria and a music performance space should be avoided if at all possible.

Left: An acoustical shell is essential for effective music performance on a proscenium stage. Photograph by Wenger Corporation.
Right: A pocket made of gypsum wallboard (above the door) holds the acoustical draperies retracted out of the sound field during some performances in this recital hall.

Rockville Junior and Senior High School, Rockville, Indiana. A cafetorium is an undesirable place for music performance unless it is designed first of all as a place for music performance, with proper shaping and good acoustics and lighting. Architect: Fanning, Howey Associates. Photograph by Cale and White Studio.

Common shortcomings of cafetoriums are an inadequate stage; poor acoustics; low lighting levels for performers; extremely noisy ventilating systems; poor sound isolation; and few audience amenities. Teachers who are unfortunate enough to have a cafetorium for their primary performance space can refer to recommended treatment of auditoriums and rehearsal rooms given elsewhere in this publication for ideas that may help them make the most of their room.

LARGE ASSEMBLY SPACES

Spaces such as gymnasiums or arenas can be successfully adapted for good music performance if the ceiling is of tectum or similar sound absorbing material. Without this, compensating for the "boominess" and long reverberation time is very difficult. Also, if the ceiling is very high (over twenty- to twenty-two feet) the effectiveness of the ceiling absorption is decreased and additional treatment must be located elsewhere.

Common problems in gymnasiums and arenas
- Lack of essential stage requirements
- Lack of storage space
- Poor acoustics
- Poor sight/sound lines
- Poor, inflexible lighting (both stage and audience)

Installation of thick absorptive materials with an air space behind them can be very effective in eliminating the ''boominess'' of a reverberant gymnasium.

- Noisy lighting systems
- Noisy ventilating systems
- Inadequate sound isolation from adjoining spaces
- Lack of amenities for the audience, especially in seating
- Recreational rather than artistic atmosphere
- Need for constant shifting of chairs and other equipment
- Unavoidable scheduling conflicts

This list does not completely exhaust the number of recurring problems when a gymnasium is the school performing arts center.

How to help improve gymnasiums for concerts
- Remodel the old gym into an auditorium. This has been done very successfully at a comparatively low cost and should not be ruled out too quickly as a viable option.
- Use portable staging, shells, and lighting.
- Use portable risers on stage.
- Install acoustical draperies or other acoustical materials on rear and side walls.
- Get an expert to help quiet the ventilating system.
- Experiment with placement of performers to minimize echo and reverberation by playing the ''short'' way.
- Place carpet under the players and if possible, also in front of the ensemble between performers and the audience.

Above: South Christian High School, Cutlerville, Michigan. Remodeling a gymnasium into an auditorium can be done very effectively. The open roof girders remain but the upholstered seats on a raked floor make this an excellent hall for performers and listeners alike. Architect: Daverman Associates. Acoustics: Geerdes Consulting Services.
Right: Chamber music room and classroom, Grand Rapids Junior College, Grand Rapids, Michigan. This comfortable room for chamber music and small classes is part of a former gymnasium.

REMODELING AND RENOVATION

CONVERSION PROJECTS

A shift in space can at times produce "found" space that can be adapted for music instruction at a cost considerably less than new construction. Refer to the specific space requirements in the appendix before beginning any serious planning.

Once space requirements have been determined, construction costs should be carefully analyzed to ensure that remodeling will be more cost effective than new construction. Remember that it is easier to draw lines on paper for new construction than it is to work with the bricks and mortar of existing construction. Provision for a substantial contingency item in the budget is especially advisable in remodeling and renovation projects, for unexpected costs often arise.

When conversion is recommended, large open spaces provide a flexible condition in which to build a new shell within the existing load-bearing walls. Auditoriums, gymnasiums, and some old libraries offer this possibility and allow for sufficient room height. Whether a building should or should not be converted must be examined carefully by an engineer, an architect, and an acoustical consultant, since few old buildings have sufficient foundations to bear the heavy wall construction needed for adequate sound isolation and the added weight of a heavy ceiling. In examining old facilities, internal traffic and external accessibility should be carefully reviewed. These admonitions are not intended to exclude converting or remodeling existing buildings for music purposes when the required conditions can be met. It is absolutely essential, however, to be certain that the desire for economy does not result in a facility entirely unsatisfactory for music education.

MUSIC CLASSROOMS

In America's schools, classroom music is probably taught more often in general classrooms than in rooms specifically designed for music instruction. However, remodeling presents an opportunity to upgrade the quality of these rooms to make them more suitable for their specialized usage.

Classrooms for music double as modest performance spaces (for example, classroom singing and the playing of classroom instruments) and also as primary listening areas. The best facilities will be equipped with a high-fidelity stereo disc and tape-playing system and should include a cassette and compact disc player. Compact discs have the capability to index (spot a movement or theme on a disc), and have clarity and transparency of sound. Essential requirements include permanently mounted loudspeakers and sturdy, reliable components, not overly gadgeted but with the capability to compensate for often-scratched school recordings. A videocassette

Left: Grand Rapids Junior College Music Center, Grand Rapids, Michigan. Right: Rehearsal room/recital hall, Music Center, Grand Rapids Junior College, Grand Rapids, Michigan. The gymnasium was converted into a music center. Beside the old brick building is an addition with stairways, an elevator, and quiet mechanical equipment. The rehearsal room doubles as a recital hall. The high ceiling was obtained by retaining the existing roof girders open to the room. Special acoustical panels over the rehearsal area, adjustable acoustical draperies, and a raked seating area combined to make this a functional space in an old building. Architect: Renaud Associates. Acoustics: Geerdes Consulting Services.

Below: An enlarged stage, a sloped floor for the audience seating area, side walls angled for good acoustics, and open ceiling girders to gain maximum volume make the former gymnasium work well as a high school and community auditorium.

player and a monitor that is wired to send its soundtrack through the external audio components and loudspeakers are also very desirable.

STUDIOS AND PRACTICE ROOMS

Adapting found space for private practice and teaching is especially successful when prefabricated modules are used. These are available in many sizes and shapes and offer sound isolation and room acoustics that are guaranteed by the manufacturer. Suppliers of these units offer complementary design assistance and installation.

Prefabricated rooms circumvent all hazards of on-site remodeling and construction. They can be disassembled and re-installed elsewhere if needed. Their ventilation fans produce a light sound that is useful in masking any intrusion from neighboring areas (a desirable feature in any good practice suite).

If regular on-site construction is used, installing rooms in an existing structure should be done without compromising the criteria listed earlier. Special care must be used when existing walls of dubious design are utilized, along with existing pipe and ductwork that can provide a sound path between rooms.

REHEARSAL ROOMS

Rehearsal rooms are spaces that are usually hard to accommodate successfully in a remodeling project. Particularly for high school and college instrumental groups, it is almost impossible to get the needed ceiling height that will accommodate a high sound power level. Old schoolroom conversions require a two-story height to achieve a sixteen to twenty-two foot ceiling, and structurally this might not be possible Eliminating a lowered, suspended ceiling and directly treating the bottom of the structure above can gain essential volume.

One conversion that can sometimes be done successfully is creating a music suite from an auditorium or gymnasium. Here, the main structural elements are in place and with very careful planning the requirements can be met, both in terms of area and of volume. Such a conversion taxes the skill of the facility planner and architect. Careful review of as-built blueprints (which may be hard to locate, but are very important) to identify load-bearing walls, wall mass, hidden ceiling spaces, and mechanical system details is essential. Maximum use of existing partitions will permit available funds to be used to upgrade substandard walls, improve sound isolation and quiet mechanical and electrical systems. Criteria for good rehearsal rooms are found in chapter two.

PERFORMANCE AREAS

Adopting or upgrading old performance areas to meet current standards can include converting an existing large space (such as a gymnasium into an auditorium); modernizing an old auditorium; or remodeling an open-school performance space.

CONVERTED SPACES

Most old gymnasium/auditorium combinations have an inadequate stage along the long wall. It is usually too shallow, poorly lit, and of incorrect height. Furthermore, the ventilating system was probably designed without concern for noise.

Making the stage adequate is a primary concern. In a conversion project, structural modifications that will enlarge and extend the stage must be considered. Lighting should be bright enough (seventy footcandles) for reading musical scores, with special provisions for theater stage lighting for dramatic productions. Relocating the stage to the front of a rectangular room is also often practicable, with many advantages for the audience/performer relationship.

Stage size requirements vary with the educational level, from perhaps 750 square feet in the elementary school to 1,500 to 2,000 square feet or more in the large high

Pioneer Auditorium, Michigan Public School, East Grand Rapids. This fine old auditorium was renovated with new upholstered seats, carpeted aisles, rear wall and under-balcony ceiling treatment, and new sound doors. Consultant: Geerdes Consulting Services.

school or college. Lighting requirements will also vary, but they should be carefully anticipated and incorporated into the plans, and include (if at all possible) a separate lighting and sound control room.

Audience comfort helps make attendance at school music events a pleasant experience. A sloped floor greatly improves sight and sound lines. Comfortable upholstered seats should replace metal folding chairs. Lights should be pleasant, dimmable, and quiet. Drinking fountains and adequate rest rooms and cloakrooms will be greatly appreciated. Acoustical considerations can dictate the need to alter the shape of both the stage and the audience area, and also the addition of absorptive treatment to subdue low frequencies and to improve clarity and balance. Treatment should be as close to the audience seating level as is practicable. Carpeting will add warmth and may help acoustically, although it is not an even absorber at all frequencies.

In the converted space, every effort should be made to duplicate the ideal conditions of a new facility, both in performance and support spaces. Accommodations for disabled persons must be provided. No less than one wheelchair space should be provided for each 100 seats in the auditorium. See the section on provisions for handicapped persons on pages 58–59.

MODERNIZATION

Old auditoriums are generally structurally sound and amenable to modernization, which is less expensive than new construction. The results can be very satisfactory if the project is planned carefully. A checklist of items that are usually below standard in old auditoriums follows, with some suggestions for correcting shortcomings.

Stage
- Add a demountable extension to increase size
- Install an acoustical shell and ceiling to improve hearing conditions on stage and in the audience
- Upgrade and modernize both stage and house lighting

House (audience area)
- Install comfortable seating
- Slope the floor (if possible)
- Carpet aisles and lobby
- Provide cloakrooms
- Provide adequate and convenient rest rooms and drinking fountains
- Install state-of-the-art sound reinforcement and lighting systems, including dimmers
- Provide adequate disabled accommodations

General
- Provide a manager's office
- Have adequate enough offstage storage
- Develop an orchestra pit, or a demountable railing around the orchestra area
- Review amount of lobby space
- Redecorate attractively, retaining some "classic" feeling
- Provide for handicapped accessibility
- Provide adequate and convenient parking
- Ensure that building and safety codes are followed precisely

OPEN SCHOOL PERFORMANCE AREAS

An open school may have had a separate rehearsal room, but it was usually designed without an enclosed space for performances. The need for quiet was violated, walking through the area could usually not be avoided, and most of the desirable conditions of privacy, quiet, comfortable seating, and good lighting were lacking.

Short of a major reconstruction, the situation can be improved by using temporary stage enclosures and removable stage lighting and by providing more comfortable temporary seating. The criteria stated earlier for standard performance spaces should be reviewed and as many improvements as possible should be applied to the open situation.

CHAPTER 7

COLLEGE AND UNIVERSITY MUSIC FACILITIES

The arts provide an additional important medium of expression beyond that of the printed word. Their unique nature makes specialized facilities for them essential, especially in institutions of higher learning. Every effort should be made to make each music room fully supportive of every activity carried on within it. College facilities should provide an ideal against which music education students can assess the adequacy of their future school facilities. Audiences should hear performances that sound their best, and are enhanced by the environment.

For these and other reasons, planning a music facility for an institution of higher learning presents a particular set of challenges. The teaching staff is larger, making a larger support staff necessary, and space is needed to accommodate all of the special functions. The larger universities may have their own architectural staffs that can exert a strong influence on the plans for a new building even though they may lack experience in its highly specialized requirements. Also, public school building projects are generally funded by the school district out of tax revenues or bond issues. While this may be true of some college and university projects, it is not uncommon for them to require additional funding sources. Often this introduces a major donor into the planning picture who can be a strong but disruptive force in constructing a functional building.

Private colleges often fund new music quarters through special development campaigns. These often require architectural renderings of a still unprogrammed or unplanned structure. This can compromise the final product. Good music buildings cost much more per square foot than regular school buildings. Unless the architect has considerable experience designing music buildings, the per-square-foot preliminary cost estimate will be much too low. So, the funding goals are frequently unrealistically low and the success of the building is easily compromised even before it is fully planned.

Engaging a music planning consultant very early in the planning process can relieve the department chairman of many responsibilities. The consultant can also guide the planning from its earliest steps of programming and delineating space requirements on through the completed design and final construction, including the technical details involved in layout, noise control, and room acoustics.

Should the consultants for the planning, acoustical, and other areas be chosen and hired by the institution or by the architect? While it can work satisfactorily either way, there are certain advantages to having the college hire consultants directly. This saves the normal markup that the architect is obliged to add to any specialist's fee. More important, the consultant hired by the college becomes its advocate and

Fine Arts Center, Calvin College, Grand Rapids, Michigan. College and university music facilities should serve as models for future teachers. Architects: The Perkins & Will Partnership, Daverman Associates. Acoustics: Artec Consultants.

representative throughout the planning and construction process. The consultant reports each recommendation to administrators as well as to the architect and sees that it is followed. Such an adviser can be an invaluable member of the planning and design team and can continue to monitor the project through completion of construction.

College and university music facilities often provide space for extra school needs of the community. To do this well, such community use must be carefully planned, with special extra storage for nonschool equipment. For example, if the local symphony orchestra rehearses at the college, secure music and instrument storage is required. Also, the facility should have easily accessible and adequate parking.

Facilities that combine the fine arts work well for institutions of higher learning. Since exposing students and patrons of music to theater and the visual arts is a broadening experience that offers many challenging possibilities for the arts to interact, concentrating the arts into one facility (though it makes planning more complex) can result in a more interesting and vital building.

A fine arts building requires an office for a building manager and staff. Scheduling, staffing, and specialized maintenance are just a few of the important duties of this manager who needs an office (preferably located within the building) to work effectively. Without it, full and efficient use of the facility and its technical resources is unlikely.

Another important consideration is that of building equipment. It is complicated by the variety of needs as compared with those of a nonmusic classroom building, and also by the number of faculty members, each having unique requirements. Planning a new building seems to stimulate unrealistic requests, so a useful approach is to develop two lists, one "absolutely must have," and another "it would be nice to have," with budgets for each level. Although funding the equipment budget is usually done outside the building budget, it is no less important to equip it well than it is to plan and build it well.

College teaching studios should be designed with optimum acoustics, adjustable if possible.

Institutions of higher learning will serve their students best if their facilities for the musical arts can serve as a model for future teachers. Such structures should meet the criteria listed in earlier chapters more stringently than is generally true in schools. The emphasis should always be on the cardinal precept that the rooms in which music teaching and learning occur are extensions of the voices or instruments and thus are of crucial importance. This means that the various elements of good design, including the following, should be close to the ideal:

● Room acoustics
● Sound containment and isolation
● Good, quiet lighting
● Adequate, quiet ventilation

The college and university music suite should have good traffic patterns, high enough rehearsal room ceilings, convenient storage and adequate support spaces. Unique to the college situation is the desirability of a student lounge for socializing and relaxing between lessons, classes, and rehearsals. It should not only be comfortable but pleasant and spacious since it can contribute immeasurably to the esprit de corps of the music department.

STUDIOS AND PRACTICE ROOMS

On the college level, one-on-one teaching is an essential and basic component of the music program, increasing the need for more and better individual practice rooms and teaching studios than are found in secondary schools. The number of studios, which usually double as faculty offices, corresponds directly to the number of applied music students and teachers. Unlike nonmusic offices, music offices cannot be shared since the college teacher must have the studio available for practicing and professional work at all times. The studios should be designed with optimum in-room acoustics that may include nonparallel walls and wall panels customized for each studio. Good sound isolation between studios is critical. Double walls with an airspace filled with special dense, sound-absorbing material is one way to achieve sound isolation. Careful attention must be given to caulking all joints and wall penetrations to make them airtight and sound tight.

If a private teacher coaches chamber ensembles such as string quartets or woodwind quintets, the studio/office should be large enough to accommodate rehearsals unless there is an accessible and adequate small ensemble rehearsal room. The studio/office should house music files, record and book storage shelves, a desk, and such other needed equipment. Individual requirements such as chalkboards, bulletin boards, mirrors, and a coat rack should be reviewed carefully with each teacher, and every effort should be made to accommodate the staff so they can teach in their studio with maximum pleasure and effectiveness.

If money is not available to build both individual practice rooms and teaching studios with maximum acoustics and sound control, the studios (where teachers spend many hours each day) should receive the best possible treatment. Student practice rooms, which are generally occupied for one hour at a time, can be compromised somewhat, but with provisions for improving their sound isolation at a later time when funds are available. This is also an alternative for an existing building, where upgrading the rooms can effectively be done later.

Because of the emphasis on private study, colleges require excellent smaller performance spaces for recitals and small ensemble performances. These needs are accommodated in recital halls (see page 41). An open stage that places performers and listeners in a single, unified room is ideal for college-level recitals. Seating from 150–250 people, it can be an ideal, intimate venue for soloists and chamber groups alike.

MUSIC LISTENING CENTERS

One facility usually found at the college level is a music listening center. It can be located in the music suite—convenient to music classrooms—or within the library, since it is a learning resource center that includes score study and music listening.

The music listening center is a unique area that requires specific, careful layout, considerable sound absorption to maintain quiet conditions, and precise design of the electronic elements. If it is located convenient to music classrooms, both areas can share the same records, tapes, scores, and video materials. Operation by library personnel during the extended hours the library is open relieves the music department of the cost and staffing problems of a center in music department quarters. A listening center should also be equipped as a viewing center for televised materials.

A good listening center should include:

- A control area or room housing a custom-designed switch bank that chooses from multiple sources and sends the material to a selected listening station or stations.
- Sources should include compact discs, record albums, cassette tapes, reel-to-reel tapes, FM radio, television, and a videocassette recorder (VCR) and player. The VCR should be in the VHS format, since more music videos are available in VHS than Beta.
- Individual listening stations equipped with high-quality stereo headsets, independent volume control, and a work area that can hold scores or notebooks.
- Equipment that filters surface noise and scratches on old recordings in the collection so memorable performances by great artists are preserved in a passable listening condition.

REHEARSAL AND PERFORMANCE ROOMS

College and university rehearsal and performance rooms should meet (and if possible, exceed) the criteria for those of a large high school (see Appendix). The auditorium should match the conditions found in major concert halls. Even in large institutions, every effort should be made to limit the seating capacity of the auditorium

Above: Taylor University, Upland, Indiana. This listening center incorporates ten audio sources that can be channelled into one to twenty listening stations or to an adjoining classroom.

Left: The control panel is designed for simple operation by student assistants. Video projection to monitors in the adjoining learning resource center or the classroom is also possible. Architect: The Troyer Group. Consultant: Geerdes Consulting Services. Electronics: Ascom.

Towsley Center, School of Music, University of Michigan, Ann Arbor. Architects: TMP Associates. Acoustical consultant: R. Lawrence Kirkegaard & Associates. Photograph by Balthazar Korab.

A better space for student performers can be designed for 1,000 or 2,000 than for any larger. Performances in a small hall can be repeated in order to accommodate a larger audience. (The repeat performances, in fact, can be beneficial to student performers.) The auditorium should be considered a laboratory for the performing arts and as such the stage and its equipment are much more important than the number of seats.

ORGAN STUDIOS

The organ studio is unique to college and university music departments. The studio should be large enough to hold a pipe organ having at least eight to ten ranks of pipes. The room should seat twenty or thirty (for studio classes), with the possibility of additional seating if it is also to be used as an organ recital hall. Ideally, it should have a large volume and live acoustics. This means careful shaping of the walls, avoiding concave surfaces that focus sounds, and careful design of ceiling elements. The goal of maintaining clarity and brilliance can easily produce a room that rings and has flutter echoes, and that may require careful placement of absorptive material on one or two adjoining walls.

The organ studio floor should be at least fifteen by twenty-five feet, have nonparallel walls (convex shaping is advised), and the ceiling should be approximately twenty-two feet high. Suspended sound-reflective panel should be installed sixteen to eighteen feet above the floor, and have a sound-absorbing blanket above them. Carpeting should be avoided unless it is needed to help quiet an overly reverberant space where other, more desirable options do not seem practicable.

It is wise for the college to have a variety of organs available for hands-on training, such as mechanical tracker action organs, electro-pneumatic action, or electronic instruments for students whose careers could very well include playing any of these types in addition to the pipe organ.

CHAPTER 8

EQUIPMENT

A poorly equipped music department cannot progress at the desired rate no matter how excellently it is housed. Directors can be seriously hindered by the lack of proper equipment. An important rule in purchasing any school equipment is to *buy something good and then take care of it*. New furniture and equipment developments should be reviewed right up to delivery.

INSTRUMENTS

Piano

Upright pianos can be used in music rooms for rehearsals, but a grand piano should be available for major musical activities. It is always advisable to purchase the largest possible piano that the budget will allow. Tone quality depends on the size of the sounding board area and the length of the strings (for the lower tones). The keyboard height and pedal height for both upright and grand pianos should be the same. Many manufacturers are incorporating plastic bushings, but these have not proved to be satisfactory. For school pianos, good wooden action parts and felt bushings still give the best service. Upright pianos that are to be moved should be mounted on large rubber ball-bearing casters, or on piano gliders equipped with this type of caster. Grand pianos should be mounted on a glider that does not raise so high that operation of the pedals is difficult.

It is not advisable to purchase inexpensive pianos because they will receive heavy use over a long period. A poorly constructed piano cannot produce desirable tone quality, often does not hold its tuning, and is not dependable mechanically. With the aid of staff and consultants, each school can make its own specifications for pianos when requesting bids. In preparing such specifications, consideration should be given to overall size, cabinet and finish, casters, key bed, keys, plate, back and pin plank, tuning pins, sounding board, ribs, bridges, action, and musical tone. In addition, special conditions may necessitate keyboard cover locks, special sized racks, dust covers, or other items. All pianos should be tuned to A-440 three or four times a year. It is unfair to ask students to listen to or perform on a piano when it needs tuning.

Electronic pianos are finding increasing favor with schools and colleges for class piano instruction and theory classes. The expense of a system with six electronic pianos is less than the cost of a grand piano. Their use is discussed in chapter two.

Organ

Decisions regarding organs must be based on the music department's objectives and, to some extent, the educational level of the students using the facilities: whether an organ will be installed in a recital hall; whether there will be a teaching studio or practice room equipped with an organ; and whether the organ will be electronic or pipe. The planner should not purchase an electronic instrument without investigating the possibility of a small pipe organ, at least in the recital hall or auditorium. Whenever possible, students should be educated on authentic instruments. In some situations, however, the electronic organ is the only alternative. If this is the case, an electronic organ should be selected with stops and voicing that parallel the traditional pipe organ.

Band and orchestra instruments

A complete listing of instruments that should be provided by the institution can be found in the Appendix.

AUDIOVISUAL EQUIPMENT

Supplying a new music facility with audiovisual equipment can require considerable expense to which the cost of stocking magnetic videotape, transparencies, and films must be added. Equipment maintenance and repair also must be budgeted. Careful planning should be done to ensure that equipment will be used regularly by the music teacher, and that adequate funds will be budgeted to provide for audiovisual needs.

TAPE RECORDING

Anything written today about the subject of electronics is apt to be obsolete by the time it appears in print. Spectacular developments in miniaturization, use of solid-state components, and advanced technologies have brought this about. Tape recorders (especially cassette units) allow students to record their playing, listen to a professional performance, or have a permanent record of a performance of an original composition. Classes can be recorded and used at the student's convenience. Performance recordings can be used to improve interpretation, tone quality, balance, and technique. The student must use high-quality equipment to ensure maximum usability. Poor equipment will defeat the the intended purpose. Only professional equipment should be purchased by schools, since theirs is a professional use in every sense of the word. Although the quality of discount outlets has improved considerably, the music educator should contact a professional audio dealer for advice, selection, and installation of equipment. If an audio consultant is retained to design the auditorium sound system, he or she can then draw up specifications for recording and listening equipment for the rest of the building. Specifications presented in this section should be considered as minimal, since future equipment undoubtedly will be better. Digital audio tape, for example, will soon equal the quality of compact discs, so equipment that utilizes this technology should be considered for your facility.

Magnetic tape

A tape system consists of two elements: the magnetic tape and its transport with the associated electronics. Both are fundamental parts of the system, and a compromise on either will produce inferior results. This is true of both reel-to-reel and cassette recorders. Use standard brand-name tape. "White box" tape often is sold with a private brand name at a reduced price, but it should not be used because it often is made for other purposes (such as substandard computer tape), and may deposit excessive oxide on tape heads and drive units, or be unlubricated or excessively abrasive.

Open-reel tape is supplied on five-, seven-, or ten-inch reels. Smaller reels than these are not practical for high-quality machines. Length of tape on the reel is determined both by its diameter and by the thickness of the tape. Tapes less than 1 mil thick should be avoided, with 1½ mil tapes being standard. A seven-inch reel of the former yields forty-five minutes of recording time at 7½ ips or ninety minutes at

3¾ ips; 1½ mil tapes give thirty minutes at 7½ ips or sixty minutes at 3¾ ips. The thinner tapes not only are difficult to handle and prone to breakage, but also store poorly and tend to aggravate print-through or other problems. If a tape is to be used only for study purposes, a good general-purpose tape is sufficient. If, however, the recording will be used to make phonograph records, it should be made on low-noise tape. Assignments for listening centers using student-operated equipment should be recorded on extra-strength tapes that resist wear and breakage. Mylar-based tapes may stretch if subjected to hard handling or if used on a machine that is poorly adjusted. (Stretching renders a tape unusable.) It is better to have a tape break than to have it stretch, since broken tapes can be repaired.

For many years, magnetic tapes were made of fine particles of iron oxide adhered to an acetate or mylar base. New formulas have been developed that use chromium oxide to improve the recording characteristics available at slower speeds. Other new coatings are in the developmental stage. Cassette tapes offer fewer options than reel-to-reel tape, but they also are available in different thicknesses and lengths. The thirty-minute cassette tape (in one direction) is standard. These tapes, which are thicker and more durable than forty-five minute tapes (in each direction), should be used unless they are to be subjected to infrequent use. Digital audio tapes will be available on smaller cassettes that offer extended playing times and better fidelity.

REEL-TO-REEL RECORDERS

Reel-to-reel tape recorders are less popular today than formerly because of the convenience and improved fidelity of cassette recordings. But schools should not be without a reel-to-reel machine because of its ease of editing and splicing, which is not available in any other medium. Also, most schools have a sizable collection of existing tapes in their libraries that would be inaccessible without an appropriate playback unit. A wide range of so-called "professional" tape recorders are available. Unfortunately, the word "professional" has been misused, and the prospective buyer should

Only professional recording equipment should be considered for educational use.

be wary of misrepresentation. Even published specifications should be viewed with some skepticism, since important elements are often omitted. A reliable dealer or audio consultant can demonstrate the equipment and point out desirable features. In general, the faster the tape speed, the better the fidelity. Machines today can record at 7½ ips with a fidelity achieved only at 15 or 30 ips twenty years ago. Even 3¾ ips on certain machines is now acceptable for all but the most critical uses. A reel capacity of seven inches is adequate, although a ten-inch reel offers twice the uninterrupted recording time. Frequency response should be flat ± two decibels from 30 to 15,000 Hz, with a signal-to-noise ratio of sixty decibels and flutter and wow measurements not over 0.15.

Tape recorders are practical because they are easy to operate, transport, and store, and sensible use keeps maintenance costs to a minimum. Preventive maintenance must be performed at recommended intervals, and tape heads and drive mechanisms must be kept scrupulously clean. Tape machines with internal amplifiers and loudspeaker systems are not satisfactory for music department use. A separate tape deck, amplifier, and loudspeakers are required. At one time, full-track monaural recordings using the complete one-quarter-inch width of the tape were considered necessary for excellent quality reproduction. With the advent of stereo, two channels were recorded simultaneously, each channel using one-half the tape width. For the narrow tape widths required by small cassettes, very narrow recording tracks now are producing excellent fidelity with a good signal-to-noise ratio. This is due in part to the development of noise reduction systems, such as Dolby, which should be included.

CASSETTE RECORDERS

Cassette decks are available that, when played through an external amplifier and speaker system, can exceed the quality of disc recordings. Quality cassette recorders can now meet specifications that once were reserved for professional open-reel tape machines. Variable pitch control is a useful feature, and a dual-cassette machine offers a convenient way to make copies of rehearsal and concert tapes (some machines can duplicate at double speed).

DIGITAL RECORDING

The tape system of the future will be digital recording and playback using a system that digitally extracts noise and hiss leaving only the pure audio signal, which is then coded onto tape in digital form by a method much like that used to store computer information. This means that the music teacher will have available tape recordings with uncannily quiet backgrounds and the purest, cleanest, and most natural music ever heard on tape. How much more effectively can we present the world's great music to our students than through the latest, most advanced systems available? They should be a part of every school's music department.

PCM RECORDING

"PCM" (Pulse Code Modulation) is one of the newer techniques that has come into widespread professional use and is practicable for schools, too. It is a form of digital tape recording that is easy to use and digitally "perfect." Electrical impulses are converted to numbers (digits) for recording and the reverse in replay, which increases the signal-to-noise ratio so tapes have much lower noise levels and extended dynamic range equal to that of the compact disc. For PCM recording, two pieces of equipment are required: a PCM processor and a standard videocassette recorder (VCR) that is a regular VHS or Beta unit that can be used for video recording as well. Disadvantages to the system are equipment cost, no editing/splicing features, and the rarity of processors available to students. It is very likely that the new DAT (Digital Audio Tape) systems will render the PCM out-of-date for school use because of the lower cost, editing capabilities, and widespread acquisition by consumers for home use.

COMPACT DISC PLAYERS

The clarity and fidelity of their music reproduction and the ability to "index"—move to specific points on the disc allowing the teacher to pinpoint themes and movements—make compact disc players ideal for music instruction. In the future, the compact disc will replace the long-playing record as the medium of choice, just as the long-playing record replaced the 78-rpm record. They become increasingly desirable as the repertoire available on them increases and their cost declines. Indefinite wear with no deterioration in tone quality, and no scratches or clicks help place the listener closer to the source. Realism and naturalness without an audible intervening medium make listening a genuine and authentic musical experience.

LISTENING CENTERS

The music listening center parallels the foreign language laboratory in offering new approaches to education. Programmed materials that allow self-instruction in ear training are readily available on tape. Student practice can be monitored for later evaluation by the student himself or the instructor. Selections can be taped for students in music history and appreciation classes. Listening centers can be as simple or as complex as available space and money allow since they are usually custom-designed for the particular installation. These are discussed in chapters two and seven.

RECORD PLAYERS

Phonograph records have advantages over reel-to-reel tapes and cassettes for certain educational uses. They are more easily handled for class use since the instructor can skip selections more easily than with tape. Records are disadvantageous from the standpoint of wear and distortion. Even with proper care, a heavily used record deteriorates in quality. On either turntables or record changers, a cuing lever for the tone arm is especially useful. Diamond styluses are the only practical kind for school use. When used carefully in a tone arm with light tracking force, they can withstand many weeks of frequent use. A stylus microscope to check for wear is a worthwhile accessory. Replacement styluses should be made by the manufacturer of the cartridge.

FM RADIO

A large number of high-fidelity educational radio stations now broadcast throughout the United States, usually featuring many hours of serious music programming each day. In some large metropolitan areas, there are also commercial FM stations presenting similar programs. The possibility of tape-recording broadcasts for use at a more convenient time also is an appealing feature. Most stations can provide a list of scheduled performances several weeks in advance to facilitate this process. Addition of an FM radio tuner to the recording or playback system requires a very modest investment compared with its potential value to the school music program since it can use the existing amplifier and speakers. The desirability of a recording/broadcasting control booth is discussed in chapter four. This booth is the ideal location for an FM tuner if it is not located in the school office as part of the master intercom system. From the sound control booth, programs can be broadcast to the school system.

CLASSROOM PLAYBACK SYSTEMS

Playback systems for music classrooms, rehearsal rooms, or teaching studios should be designed with careful consideration of their planned use. With the many options available using record albums, reel-to-reel tapes, cassettes, and compact discs a system can become too complex for convenient use. Mounting the players and controls in a portable cabinet on casters can make the system readily accessible. A self-

Playback systems for classroom and studio use may be on casters with permanent loudspeakers mounted on the wall.

coiling cord carrying audio and electrical connections is helpful. Classroom playback systems should have both record-playing and reel-to-reel tape-playing capabilities, as well as the ability to play compact discs, which are ideal for classroom use. Tape decks without recording amplifiers are adequate for these rooms. Systems should have stereophonic electronics, and the loudspeakers ideally should be wall-mounted with concealed wiring and spaced eight to ten feet apart, depending on the size of the room.

Tape-recording capabilities for rehearsal rooms and private teaching studios allow rehearsals and lessons to be taped and reviewed by teacher and pupils. All the audio components in each system must be compatible and of relatively equal quality. One low-quality component will reduce the effect of all other components. A professional audio engineer can offer wise counsel on matching the units of the system and installing cassette players or radio tuners as well as the basic record, compact disc and tape players. The system should have enough power-handling capacity to serve the room in which it is located.

AUDITORIUM PLAYBACK SYSTEMS

Auditorium playback systems should be independent of the sound reinforcement system but at least equal in quality to it. The reasons for this are that the sound amplification system usually is controlled from the rear of the auditorium, where it is not accessible to someone teaching or playing records on stage or at the front of the hall, and that the sound system usually is monaural. For maximum flexibility, the auditorium playback system should be movable, with the component cabinet and loudspeakers each mounted on large casters. A stereophonic record player, compact disc, tape, and cassette units should be incorporated into this system, with enough power to fill the entire hall at high level if necessary. This does not exclude the possibility of playing tapes, records, or compact discs through the auditorium sound system.

CENTRAL SOUND SYSTEMS

The equipment by which radio programs and announcements are distributed throughout the school usually is shared by the entire building and therefore is only partially the responsibility of the music department. Most systems are equipped so that classrooms can be monitored from the central switchboard, so that the equipment can be used as a two-way communication system between classrooms and office. All equipment should be purchased from a well-established manufacturer and installed by engineers experienced in such work. Even so, the best of these systems is suitable only for carrying spoken announcements or background music, and the music teacher should resist attempts to use this system for serious music reproduction. The small speakers that are satisfactory for spoken announcements are inadequate for music reproduction.

PORTABLE PUBLIC ADDRESS SYSTEMS

Portable systems usually are shared with other departments. Since this equipment may be used for outdoor band concerts and musical performances in auditoriums not permanently equipped, the same supervision should be exercised in its selection as for a central system. Microphones should be high quality, and the amplifiers should have sufficient reserve power to reproduce music without distortion. A fifty-watt amplifier is the absolute minimum for use outdoors and in large auditoriums. High-quality speakers mounted in bass-reflex baffles generally are most satisfactory for musical purposes provided that extreme volume is unnecessary and that problems of microphone placement do not accentuate their tendency toward feedback. In conditions involving these difficulties, horn-type speakers may be necessary, but they must be selected with great care because many horn-type speakers have poor fidelity. The light, self-contained, battery-powered megaphone is of considerable use in drilling the marching band. It is of no use for musical amplification, but its extreme portability and ease of operation make it a valuable rehearsal aid.

MONITORING SYSTEMS

Where a number of practice rooms are used at one time, the teacher should be able to supervise them all from his office. This is accomplished by an inexpensive intercom system that has a switchboard installed in the director's office. Since it will be used primarily for casual inspection, a system using a compact loudspeaker that can be reversed and used as a microphone is adequate. A number of other uses can be suggested by the engineers supplying such equipment.

TUNING DEVICES

The standard tuning bar for instrumental rooms has given way to its electronic counterpart. The electronic tuner has the advantages of added volume, variable pitch, and continuous sound. Transistorized, battery-operated models free the tuner from the electrical cord and require no warm-up time. Some models incorporate a convenient metronome. Tuning stroboscopes, both chromatic and single pitch, are available for school use and are helpful in teaching and checking intonation. A visual indication of pitch is given, and the student can see when he is in tune. Its greatest potential value to the instrumental department is for personal work in overcoming intonation problems on an individual instrument. It should not be used as a substitute for ear training and tuning by ear in full rehearsal. The device may have other uses in the music and physics departments. Other electronic instruments have been developed to train students in judging intonation. Some can reproduce the entire chromatic scale in one or more octaves. Others are keyboard operated and permit adjustment of

Left: A complete synthesizer system for school use should include a digital sequence decoder (top left), an FM sound generator (top right), a multitrack cassette recorder (bottom left), and a rhythm composer in addition to the synthesizer keyboard. Its own stereo loudspeakers are mounted on the posts, or the signal can be routed through an existing playback system. Right: Electronic keyboards may have very specialized and different functions. Top to bottom are a digital wave synthesizer, a digital sampling keyboard, and a sampled piano that has tonal options including acoustic or electronic piano, marimba, vibraphone, or clavinet as well as an electric or acoustic bass.

various intervals and tuning to just or tempered scales. Another electronic device visualizes volume levels. Better engineered, miniaturized, and more highly portable electronic tuning devices are continually being made available.

METRONOMES

In addition to spring-driven, pendulum-type metronomes, there also are many electric models available. Variably timed pulsations are obtained by simply adjusting the dial. In addition to an aural click, some have a blinking light. If there is a large volume of sound, such as in percussion practice, this visual indication is needed. There are also metronomes that will produce multiple-beat patterns simultaneously. A pocketwatch-sized windup metronome or transistorized miniature unit is useful for checking tempi of processionals or marching bands.

OTHER ELECTRONIC EQUIPMENT

Many other electronic devices are available for a variety of specialized uses. Among them are rhythm and pitch training machines, electronic "blackboards," synthesizers and electronic keyboards, and a host of other units designed to aid various aspects of music instruction. While some of them may be considered gadgets, many of them are of genuine value to music instruction at all levels.

COMPUTERS

No electronic teaching aid can equal the computer in importance. New ways to use it and more programs are being developed rapidly, and it is becoming an almost indispensable tool for music learning. Correctly used, computers can, among other things:

- Appeal to youngsters as a familiar tool from general education, where it is widely used.
- Stimulate interest in music learning.
- Reinforce other learning methods.
- Develop musical abilities.
- Facilitate acquisition of routine facts and skills.
- Print out music compositions.

To use a computer, you need *hardware*, which is the computer itself, and *software*, which consists of programs to run the system.

The hardware includes:

- A central processor unit (CPU), which includes a *disk drive* and *diskettes*.
- The disk drive, which stores information on disks much like a tape recorder store music or speech.
- The *diskettes*, often called "floppy disks," which are coated plastic disks that store information.
- A *monitor*, a screen for viewing the material being processed.
- A *keyboard*, on which information can be entered.
- An *interface card*, or better, a MIDI interface (Musical Instrument Digital Interface), which allows the computer and electronic music devices to communicate as well as play and record music.
- A *MIDI keyboard*, which permits you to play music through an interface (connector) on the computer.
- A *printer*, which prints on paper the computer's output, such as letters, graphs, drawings, and musical scores.
- An *amplifier* (needed only if the music keyboard lacks built-in loudspeakers); stereo amplifier and speakers can also be used.

A good computer includes its own instructions (thus minimizing reliance on printed manuals), which include step-by-step instructions on how to carry out each program.

The software is almost limitless in variety. It is stored on floppy disks and gives instructions to the computer for the various programs. Not all software is interchangeable with computers of different makes, so often the choice of computer must be made on the basis of the software available to use with it. This cannot be stressed strongly enough to the neophyte in the computer field: Never invest in a computer until you have made absolutely certain that the program you intend to use are indeed available to work with a particular computer. Some very popular personal computers have little usable software for music educators. Fortunately, there are others with exciting new programs being added to their libraries regularly. Be sure to check this out carefully.

Left: A computer used for music production includes music keyboard, typewriter keyboard, cassette interface (for storage or retrieval of music and other data), and a floppy disk drive.
Right: A synthesizer hooked up with a MIDI to other electronics that are, if effect, "a music keyboard in a box." The possibilities for voice programming, transposition, function selection, and other creative uses are almost limitless.

Also be aware that much of what is being written today about the computer in music education and electronic instruments and equipment for teaching will very likely be out of date by the time it appears in print. So try to get current information on this exploding field. We can safely predict that the newer generations of computers will use a 3½'' floppy disk for storage rather than the old 5¼'' format. These smaller disks can hold more information, which means the inconvenience of changing disks occurs less frequently. Also, they are less easily damaged, which is an important advantage over the old disks. This is particularly true in schools where they are vulnerable to oily fingerprints and dust that can wreck a disk and void a program. If you already have a 5¼'' disk drive, you can get an inexpensive adapter cable that makes it possible to transfer your programs to the new smaller disk.

As new electronic equipment evolves, we will find some of the individual components of a computer system integrated into others so that fewer units and simpler hook-ups are required. The adaptation of computer techniques to the needs of music educators will continue to present new opportunities to improve the teaching techniques of creative teachers in a progressive school environment.[10]

PROJECTORS

Whether a part of the music department or the audiovisual department equipment, a good 16mm sound projector is essential. Many excellent music films are available. The equipment should have the capability of being played through listening equipment in the room.

Projectors for slides and filmstrips are available separately or in combination. For school purposes, the combination units may be the most desirable. Modern lantern slide projectors (three and one-half inches by four inches) are available. The advantages of the overhead projector have made it a widely used piece of equipment in recent years. Transparencies can be made by using properly equipped photocopiers. Opaque projectors, though much improved, still require a darkened room. Improved models now can project a sheet of music up to eight and one-half by eleven inches. Video reproduction of computer-generated music is another intriguing possibility.

VIDEO MONITORS AND SCREENS

Because of the size of the viewing audience, the method of viewing television programs in the classroom, rehearsal hall, or auditorium becomes a major concern. Large monitors with conventional screens (but no receiving capability) are acceptable for classroom use. Larger spaces can benefit from use of a video projector that can be positioned either in front of or behind a screen. Technology is being developed that will produce large-screen projection at an affordable cost for schools. With the audio channeled through an external sound system, overall excellent reproduction of both sight and sound is possible.

AUDIOVISUAL SCREENS

Certain rooms in the music suite should be provided with wall or ceiling-mounted audiovisual screens, with portable screens available for other locations. The size and shape of the screens is determined by room and audience size as well as the type of projector. In planning the location of the screen, remember that the beam of light must strike the screen at a 90° angle to avoid distortion. Enough space must be allowed at the front of the room so that no one is less than two screen widths away. If the auditorium has a proscenium arch, it should be high enough to accommodate a

---

10. For more information on the rapidly growing field of computer-assisted instruction, refer to the December 1986 issue of the *Music Educators Journal*.

screen whose width is approximately one-sixth the depth of the audience area. Controls for raising and lowering auditorium screens should be located in the projection area as well as backstage.

DUPLICATING EQUIPMENT

The music department in a large school may not find it satisfactory to rely on the duplicating equipment that serves the entire school. Because of new copying methods, the old spirit duplicator is considered obsolete in most schools. However, it does provide fast, inexpensive, purple copies for class use. The mimeograph can still provide inexpensive and relatively attractive black-and-white copies. An offset press or multilith is a possibility for large departments, but due to cost is usually limited to purchase by the entire school system rather than a single department. However, the ubiquitous photocopy machine is hard to match for speed and convenience. (Copyright violation through the use of the photocopy machine has been widespread, and the Music Educators National Conference has taken a firm stand in cautioning its membership to avoid any illegal copying of copyrighted music scores or other material.)

FURNITURE AND OTHER EQUIPMENT

Music stands

Schools should purchase high-quality, durable, nonfolding telescopic stands with nonbreakable bases. The number of stands for an instrumental group can be estimated at a ratio of 1:1½. Extra stands are needed for practice rooms. Students may have to provide their own folding music stands for special appearances when school music stands cannot be easily transported.

Chairs and chair stands

High-quality nonfolding posture chairs are recommended for music seats. Comfort should be a major consideration, but the chairs must encourage students to sit erect. Chair legs should have rubber tips or rounded metal plates to protect the floors. A shelf under each chair can store books and music if needed. Chairs for singers should provide back support. Cellists should have chairs that permit them to sit on the forward edge. Specially designed posture chairs always are preferable to regular seating. These are available with drop or removable tablet arms.

String bass players should use stools that are approximately thirty inches high or use adjustable metal chair stands that have footrests and adjustable pin cups. Similar specially designed chair stands for tuba and sousaphone help hold the heavy and cumbersome instrument in correct playing position and provide convenient and safe storage. An adjustable swivel stool is desirable for the tympanist.

Conductor's podium

The podium should be movable and constructed to match the room or stage. The minimum size is approximately eight inches high and two and one-half inches to three inches square. For large choral or instrumental groups, a two-step podium sixteen inches high with an eight-inch step on each side may be desired. For safety, the top should be covered with corrugated vinyl tread or for greater comfort, a piece of rubber-backed carpeting. Metal gliders placed on the corners will prevent scratching the floor. Large podiums should be provided with cutouts or handles for easy carrying. Factory-made podiums are available in either moveable or fixed units.

Many school conductors prefer to be seated during rehearsals. A podium chair stand has an adjustable padded swivel seat and built-in podium that permits standing while conducting. An oversized music rack is useful, and this can be combined with a folio storage cabinet or even tape- and record-playing equipment if desired.

Risers

Various kinds of risers are an important part of the equipment for any music department. The merits of built-in or movable risers in rehearsal rooms is discussed in chapter two. If risers will be built in (in spite of the strictures their use places on an instrumental room), their width and location are critical. Too great a width wastes space and spreads out the performers more than they would be on a flat floor. If the school does not have an orchestra, riser widths of forty-eight inches is adequate for a single row of instrumentalists playing wind instruments. Space requirements for a row of flutes or clarinets, for example, are much different from those for a row of cellos or bass viols. The top riser should be up to 120 inches wide since the back of the room ordinarily accommodates the larger percussion and bass instruments. If storage cabinets in the rear of the room have swinging doors, adequate room should be left so they can be opened when the top risers are occupied. A height of six to eight inches per step is adequate to provide good sight lines. The number of terraces can range from three to five, depending on the size of the room and the organizations using it. Risers should be positioned as far back in the room as possible so that there is plenty of space in front for the sound to mix. This also provides a convenient floor area where chamber ensembles can meet.

If portable risers are moved between rehearsal room and auditorium stage, ease of folding and moving are paramount considerations. Factory-made risers incorporate special hardware and metal in ways usually not possible if manufactured in a school shop. Lightweight aluminum is incorporated into many ready-made units to combine strength with lightness and easy maneuverability. Two sets of risers (one set for the auditorium and the other for the rehearsal hall) help avoid the logistical problems. However, instrumental directors may find the flat floor of the stage satisfactory even if risers are used in the rehearsal room. Many professional symphony orchestras have abandoned the use of risers because elevated brass and percussion sections often overbalance the strings. This may be even more true for school orchestras. However, visual aspects may override other considerations.

Risers are available for standing chorus, seated chorus, or band and orchestra. Dimensions and capacities are readily available in suppliers' and manufacturers' catalogs. Units are available in rectangular or wedge-shaped sections to fit the dimensions of any room or stage. While risers can be built by school industrial arts or carpentry shops, such construction is no longer as popular as it once was. Because of liability laws, manufacturers are not able to make their own special hardware available separately since the proper use and assembly of this hardware is an important part of its safety. Homemade units tend to be heavy and cumbersome and take more room to store. If the risers are to be shop-built in the school in spite of these disadvantages, the catalogs should be consulted for established dimensions and riser heights. The school board must accept the legal responsibility that goes with product manufacture.

Bulletin and chalkboards

A cork board or bulletin board for official notices should be near the music director's office, built into the wall. It can be encased in glass and equipped with an inside light a lock. A bulletin board can be reserved for posting general notices, and other information. The minimum size for a bulletin board should be thirty by thirty inches.

Chalkboards (both moveable and permanent), are needed in rehearsal areas, Portable chalkboards with one slate side and one cork size have many uses in a music department. They should be light and have staff lines approximately one-inch apart with three or four inches between staves. Some manufacturers will line the boards at the factory.

Above: Solid doors, open grilles, and complete open fronts are available, with different sized compartments that can accommodate various instruments. Photograph by Wenger Corporation.

Left: Lockable individual instrument lockers can be located in hallways adjacent to rehearsal rooms or practice rooms where they will not cause traffic congestion. Open grilles permit ventilation and humidifying systems access to the individual compartments.

Sorting racks

A music sorting rack can be used equally well by vocal and instrumental organizations. Such a rack is convenient for distributing and reassembling music. A sorting rack should consist of four to five slanting shelves, one inch by fifteen inches by seventy-five inches with one inch by two inch strips at the bottom of each shelf to hold the music in place. Each shelf of the sorting rack should hold the desired number of folders, allowing two inches between folios. Two or more racks placed against the corner walls of the music library, rehearsal room, or office make it possible to use the racks conveniently. Sufficient shelf space should be provided for the greatest number of folios used by any one music organization.

Storage cabinets

The location of storage rooms is discussed in chapter two. Providing a separate space large enough to store all the instruments so the players have easy access is not always practical. Some locked storage around the periphery of the rehearsal room plus a separate, well-organized instrument room is a good combination. Additional floor space should be added to allow for cabinets and a passageway in front of them. This can add 200 to 500 square feet to the dimensions of a rehearsal room. Cabinetry in storage areas should be designed for the most efficient use of the space, provide convenient access for the user, and be safe and secure. Shelves should be large enough to accept stored items readily, but not so large that they waste space. Uncased instruments should lie on carpeted shelves to protect them from dents or scratches. Cabinets should have openings so ventilation and humidity can be kept constant.

Provision should be made for both everyday storage and permanent storage in a locked closet. A recent study revealed that most theft of school and privately owned instruments is by school employees and students. Some protection is provided by

Music folio cabinets can be custom-made to accept folders from a full section to reduce the traffic jam individual compartments can cause.

individual instrument lockers equipped with padlocks. Security has become an overriding consideration in the schools, and this aspect of the storage problem should not be minimized.

With increasing school use of amplified instruments, many music storage areas built to accommodate only traditional instruments are inadequate for power amplifiers, large loudspeaker cabinets, guitars, and other electronic equipment. Schools that use these items should plan adequate storage space for them as carefully as they do for traditional band and orchestra instruments.

Percussion cabinet

All small percussion equipment should be assembled in one space for safe storage and accessibility. The percussion cabinet should be equipped with rubber casters so that it is portable. Two of the casters should have locks to keep the stand from rolling while in use. Handles can be attached for lifting. Drop-leaf extensions on either side of the cabinet top are useful. The shelves should be designed to hold various sizes of cymbals, tom-toms, and tambourines. One shelf should be long enough to hold a set of orchestra bells. Attractive units that provide space for convenient storage, can be locked for safety, and are moved easily from rehearsal room to auditorium are available commercially.

Repair bench

Every instrumental music department should make provisions for cleaning and repairing instruments. An ideal unit includes a sink with running water, a gas unit to provide a flame, electrical outlets, a work surface, and drawers and cabinets for storing tools and supplies. The size of the repair table and the extent of its capability will depend on the mechanical interests and aptitudes of the user as well as the size of the department. Excellent ready-made repair benches with all the required facilities are available from manufacturers.

Portable shells

Portable acoustical shells frequently are necessary if musical groups are expected to perform in an auditorium with a high stage house, in a large field house, or outdoors where no permanent shell exists. The section on acoustics in chapter four discusses the requirements of shells in detail.

Sufficient weight is necessary if the panels are to reflect low and middle frequencies adequately. The surface should be hard, and panels need to be reasonably large. It is possible to meet these specifications and still maintain portability. Several commercial firms have developed a variety of shells for choral and instrumental groups. They must be counterweighted for safety, and they should be provided with casters for fast adjustability and easy movement to and from storage. Storage space easily is overlooked when a portable shell is planned. Six units that nest for storage require a space seventy-three inches high by eighty-four inches deep by seventy-six inches high. One company has a unit that combines choral risers, acoustical shell, and built-in lighting in one folding system that is both complete and convenient. Portable and mobile stages for outdoor or traveling performance (some of which combine stage and shell into a trailer that can be towed behind an automobile) are available. Custom units designed for a department's particular needs can be made to order by some equipment suppliers.

A portable shell is not intended to take the place of a regular permanent enclosure for music, especially in a proscenium-type auditorium with a high stage house. As stated in chapter four, the temptation to omit this essential piece of equipment should be resisted strenuously. However, a portable shell is better than no shell.

Music folio cabinets

Music folio cabinets for chorus, concert band, orchestra, or marching band allow students to gather their music as they enter the room and replace it as they leave. Commercially available units come in dimensions to accommodate various folios and may be combined to fit available space in the rehearsal room. Some instrumental directors prefer a music folio cabinet that will hold three to six folios in each slot to accommodate various subsections in their musical organizations.

Miscellaneous equipment

Special situations call for other types of equipment. Many elementary school music teachers have special carts fitted with rubber wheels and handles to carry songbooks, record albums, and other equipment to classrooms. Movable coat racks may be useful in some situations. A flag and stand may be required when a rehearsal area also is used as a small auditorium. Classrooms equipped with projection screens should have curtains or blinds to darken the rooms.

APPENDIX

These are excerpts from the 1986 edition of MENC's *The School Music Program: Description and Standards*.

A. ELEMENTARY SCHOOL

Facilities

The facilities provided for the music program in the elementary school meet the following standards:

Basic Program

1. A room is available for teaching general music in each school. This room has appropriate acoustical properties and is large enough to accommodate the largest group taught and provide ample space for physical movement. It also contains storage space for the necessary materials, classroom instruments, and equipment.
2. A suitable room is available for teaching instrumental music in each school. This room has appropriate acoustical properties, a quiet environment, good ventilation, and adequate lighting. It is large enough to accommodate the largest group taught and provide ample space for physical movement.

Quality Program

1. In addition to the requirements for the basic program, there is a music resource room in each school. This room is equipped for independent, self-directed study and includes at least 2 carrels with listening equipment. Its floor space is at least 1.5 times the per-pupil space allocation in the standard classroom.
2. There are 2 suitable rooms for teaching instrumental music in each school so that wind and string instruction may occur simultaneously. Each room has appropriate acoustical properties. Each room is large enough to accommodate the largest group taught with no less than 20 to 25 square feet per player. Each room is specifically designed to provide a quiet environment, room acoustics for critical listening, and lighting of no less than 40 footcandles. If the lighting is fluorescent Type A, quiet ballasts are used. Ventilation provides an exchange rate double that of

3. Sufficient secured storage space is available in each school to store the necessary instruments, equipment, and instructional materials.

4. Office space is provided for each music educator in the school.

5. The music facilities are adjacent to one another and are acoustically isolated from one another and from the rest of the school.

a regular classroom and at a low noise level.

3. In addition to the requirements for the basic program, proper lockable cabinets are provided for materials and sufficient shelving or lockers are provided for the various large and small instruments.

4. Office or studio space is provided for each music educator in the school.

5. The music facilities are adjacent to one another and are acoustically isolated from one another and from the rest of the school. In addition, the music facilities are readily accessible to the auditorium stage. The auditorium is designed acoustically for music performance. If it is a gymnasium or a cafetorium it is designed as a music space accommodating its other uses rather than the reverse. This means that consideration is given to room acoustics, noise control, and lighting so that the space is suitable for musical presentations.

B. MIDDLE SCHOOL/JUNIOR HIGH SCHOOL

Facilities

The facilities provided for the music program in grades 6–8/7–9 meet the following standards:

Basic Program

1. A room is available for teaching general music in each school. This room has appropriate acoustical properties and is large enough to accommodate the prevailing class size and provide ample space for physical movement. It also contains storage space for the necessary materials, classroom instruments, and equipment.

2. Each room in which music is taught provides an appropriate acoustical environment, with quiet and adequate lighting. Ventilation is quiet enough to allow students to hear soft music.

Quality Program

1. In addition to the requirements for the basic program, there is a music resources room in each school. This room is equipped for independent, self-directed study and includes at least 2 carrels with listening equipment. Its floor space is at least 1.5 times the per-pupil space allocation in the standard classroom.

2. Each room in which music is taught is acoustically treated to provide appropriate sound dispersion and reverberation. Each room is acoustically isolated from the rest of the school, and the vocal and instrumental areas separated by an acoustical barrier or wall with a Sound Transmission Classification (STC) of 50 or

3. Each school with more than 1 music educator contains a rehearsal room for instrumental groups and another rehearsal room for choral groups.

4. Each instrumental rehearsal room contains at least 1,800 square feet of floor space, with a ceiling at least 16 feet high and a double-entry door. Ventilation provides an air exchange rate double that of an ordinary classroom.

5. Each choral rehearsal room contains 1,200 square feet of floor space, with a ceiling at least 14 feet high and a double-entry door.

6. Each school contains an ensemble rehearsal room of at least 350 square feet.

7. Each school contains at least 1 practice room of at least 55 square feet for each 40 students enrolled in performing groups.

8. Office space of at least 55 square feet and a telephone are available for each teacher.

9. Each school contains sufficient secured storage space to store the necessary instruments, equipment, and instructional materials.

10. The music facilities in each school are adjacent to one another.

more. Noise Criterion (NC) levels of lighting and ventilating systems do not exceed NC20 for the auditorium, NC25 for music classrooms and rehearsal rooms, and NC30 for studios and practice rooms.

3. Each school with more than 1 music educator contains a rehearsal room for instrumental groups and another rehearsal room for choral groups.

4. Each instrumental rehearsal room contains at least 2,500 square feet of floor space, with a ceiling at least 20 feet high and a double-entry door. Ventilation provides an air exchange rate double that of an ordinary classroom.

5. Each choral rehearsal room contains 1,800 square feet of floor space, with a ceiling at least 16 feet high and a double-entry door.

6. Each school contains at least 2 ensemble rehearsal rooms of at least 350 square feet each.

7. Each school contains at least 1 practice room of at least 55 square feet for each 20 students enrolled in performing groups.

8. Office space of at least 55 square feet and a telephone are available for each teacher. Such space is adjacent to the rehearsal facility or instructional area in which the educator teaches and is designed so that he or she may supervise the area.

9. Each school contains sufficient secured storage space to store the necessary instruments, equipment, and instructional materials. Cabinets and shelving are provided, together with lockers for the storage of instruments in daily use. Such space is located immediately adjacent to the rehearsal facility of each group. Space is available for the repair and maintenance of instruments.

10. The music facilities in each school are adjacent to one another and are immediately accessible to the auditorium stage. The auditorium has a large open stage adaptable to the varying needs of the performing arts. The auditorium is designed with good, adjustable acoustics.

C. HIGH SCHOOL

Facilities

The facilities provided for the music program in grades 9–12 meet the following standards:

Basic Program	Quality Program

Basic Program

1. Each high school with more than 1 music educator contains a rehearsal room for instrumental groups and another rehearsal room for choral groups. If there are only 2 large rehearsal rooms, an ensemble room of at least 350 square feet is available.

2. Each instrumental rehearsal room contains at least 2,200 square feet of floor space and has a ceiling at least 16 feet high.

3. Each choral rehearsal room contains at least 1,400 square feet of floor space and has a ceiling at least 14 feet high.

4. Each high school contains at least 1 ensemble rehearsal room of at least 350 square feet.

5. Each high school contains at least 1 practice room of at least 55 square feet for each 40 students enrolled in performing groups.

6. Rehearsal and practice rooms maintain a year-round temperature range between 65 and 72 degrees with humidity between 40 and 50 percent and an air exchange rate double that of regular classrooms. At least 70 footcandles of illumination are provided. Lighting and ventilation systems are designed so that all rehearsal rooms have a Noise Criterion (NC) level not to exceed NC25; ensemble rooms, teaching studios, and electronic or keyboard rooms not to exceed NC30; and practice rooms not to exceed NC35.

7. Rehearsal rooms have double-entry doors, nonparallel or acoustically treated walls, and a sound transmission classification of at least STC50 for the interior and exterior walls and at least STC45 for doors and windows.

Quality Program

1. Separate rooms are provided for band, orchestra, and choral rehearsals, except that in small schools there may be 1 rehearsal room for instrumental groups and another rehearsal room for choral groups. If there are only 2 large rehearsal rooms, an ensemble room of at least 350 square feet is available.

2. Each instrumental rehearsal room contains at least 2,500 square feet of floor space and has a ceiling at least 20 feet high.

3. Each choral rehearsal room contains at least 1,800 square feet of floor space and has a ceiling at least 16 feet high.

4. Each high school contains at least 2 ensemble rehearsal rooms of at least 350 square feet each.

5. Each school contains at least 1 practice room of at least 55 square feet for each 20 students enrolled in performing groups.

6. Rehearsal and practice rooms can maintain a year-round temperature range between 65 and 72 degrees with humidity between 40 and 50 percent and an air exchange rate double that of regular classrooms. At least 70 footcandles of illumination are provided. Lighting and ventilation systems are designed so that all rehearsal rooms have a Noise Criterion level not to exceed NC25; ensemble rooms, teaching studios, and electronic or keyboard rooms not to exceed NC30; and practice rooms not to exceed NC35.

7. Rehearsal rooms have double-entry doors, nonparallel or acoustically treated walls, and a Sound Transmission Classification of at least STC50 for the interior and exterior walls and at least STC45 for doors and windows.

8. Each high school contains sufficient secured storage space to store the necessary instruments, equipment, and instructional materials.

9. Office space of at least 55 square feet and a telephone are available for each teacher.

10. A classroom is provided for nonperformance classes.

11. Each music classroom and rehearsal room contains at least 32 square feet of chalkboard and 24 square feet of corkboard.

12. The music facilities in each high school are adjacent to one another and are so located that they can be secured and used independently from the rest of the building.

13. The music facilities are immediately accessible to the auditorium stage. The stage is large and open and is adaptable to the varying needs of the performing arts. The auditorium is designed as a music performance space with good, adjustable acoustics, quiet mechanical systems, and adequate, quiet lighting.

8. Each high school contains sufficient secured storage space to store the necessary instruments, equipment, and instructional materials. Cabinets and shelving are provided, together with lockers for the storage of instruments in daily use. Such space is located immediately adjacent to the rehearsal facility of each group. Space is available for the repair and maintenance of instruments.

9. Office space of at least 55 square feet and a telephone are available for each teacher. Such space is adjacent to the rehearsal facility or instructional area in which the educator teaches and is designed so that he or she may supervise the area.

10. A classroom is provided for nonperformance classes, and specialized facilities are available for electronic music and piano and guitar classes.

11. Each music classroom and rehearsal room contains at least 48 square feet of chalkboard and 32 square feet of corkboard.

12. The music facilities in each high school are adjacent to one another, are immediately accessible to the auditorium stage, and are so located that they can be secured and used independently from the rest of the building.

13. The music facilities are immediately accessible to the auditorium stage. The stage is large and open and is adaptable to the varying needs of the performing arts. The auditorium is designed as a music performance space with good, adjustable acoustics for music and speech requirements, stage lighting of at least 70 footcandles, and adequate mechanical and lighting systems not to exceed a Noise Criterion level of NC20.

The musical instruments provided for the music program in grades 9–12 meet the following standards:

Basic Program

1. The following instruments are provided: 4 violins, 4 violas, 4 cellos, 4 dou-

Quality Program

1. In addition to the requirements for the basic program, the following instru-

ble basses, C piccolo, flute, 2 clarinets, 2 alto clairnets, 2 bass clarinets, 2 oboes, 2 bassoons, alto saxophone, tenor saxophone, baritone saxophone, trumpet, 4 French horns, 2 baritone horns, trombone, bass trombone, 3 tubas, 2 concert snare dums, double-tension concert bass drum, crash cymbals, suspended cymbals, 3 pedal timpani, tambourines, triangles, chimes, xylophone, marimba, orchestra bells, trap drum set, assorted percussion equipment, drum stands, movable percussion cabinet, drums for marching band if offered, enough heavy-duty music stands for the largest group, conductor's stand, music folders, tuning device, and chairs designed for music classes. Additional instruments are provided for each additional large ensemble and in situations in which students have difficulty in purchasing instruments. If class piano is taught, at least 12 acoustic or electronic pianos with console are available. If guitar is taught, at least 12 acoustic or electric guitars with control panel are available.

ments are provided: 4 violas, 4 cellos, 4 double basses, C piccolo, 2 A clarinets, E-flat clarinet, 2 alto clarinets, 2 bass clarinets, 2 contrabass clarinets, 2 oboes, English horn, 2 bassoons, 4 French horns, 2 baritone horns, bass trombone, 3 tubas, concert snare drum, pedal timpanum, marimba, vibraphone, gong, harp, electronic piano, electric bass guitar, and adequate microphones, amplifiers, and speakers for jazz ensemble and show choir.

BIBLIOGRAPHY

This bibliography includes books and articles mentioned in the text. It also gives references that will provide supplementary information on certain topics the reader may wish to pursue in greater depth. More technical details than are found in the text itself, particularly on the subjects of acoustics and sound isolation, may be explored in some of the titles enumerated here. A few of the books contain pertinent information only in certain chapters. These are obvious from their titles. A number of references are included that deal with theater planning—a subject that is considered outside the scope of this book, but that must be taken into careful consideration in planning and equipping an auditorium to accommodate both musical and theatrical performances.

BOOKS

American Association of School Administrators. *New Forms for Community Education.* Arlington, VA: AASA, 1974.

American Association of School Administrators. *Open Space Schools.* Washington, DC: AASA, 1971.

Beechold, Henry. *The Brady Guide to Microcomputer Troubleshooting and Maintenance.* Englewood, NJ: Prentice-Hall, 1987.

Beranek, Leo L. *Acoustics.* New York: American Institute of Physics, 1986.

Beranek, Leo L. *Music, Acoustics and Architecture.* New York: John Wiley and Sons, 1962. Reprint. Huntington, NY: Krieger, 1979.

Building Officials and Code Administrators Basic/National Building Code/1984. Country Club Hills, IL: BOCA, 1984.

Castaldi, Basil. *Educational Facilities, Planning, Modernization, and Management.* 3d ed. Rockleigh, NJ: Longwood Division, Allyn and Bacon, 1987.

Council of Educational Facility Planners. *Guide for Planning Educational Facilities.* Columbus, OH: CEFP, 1969.

Council of Educational Facility Planners. *What Went Wrong?* Columbus, OH: CEFP, 1968.

Cremer, Lothar, and Helmut Müller. *Principles and Applications of Room Acoustics.* 2 vols. New York and London: Applied Science Publishers, 1982.

Davis, Don. *Acoustical Tests and Measurements.* Indianapolis: Howard W. Sams and Co., 1965.

Davis, Don, and Carolyn Davis. *Sound System Engineering.* 2d ed. Indianapolis: Howards Sams/Macmillan, 1987.

Doelle, Leslie I. *Acoustics in Architectural Design.* Ottawa, Ontario: Division of Building Research, National Research Council, 1965.

Educational Facilities Laboratories. *Community/School: Sharing the Space and the Action.* New York: EFL, 1973.

Everest, F. Alton. *Successful Sound System Operation*. Blue Ridge Summit, PA: Tab Books, 1985.

Forsyth, Michael. *Buildings For Music*. Cambridge, MA: MIT Press, 1985.

Ginn, K.M. *Architectural Acoustics*. Marlborough, MA: Bruel and Kjaer Instruments, 1978.

House, Robert W. *Administration in Music Education*. Englewood Cliffs, NJ: Prentice-Hall, 1973.

Illuminating Engineering Society. *Lighting Handbook*. New York: IES, 1952.

Kehoe, Ray E. *Planning Norms and Space Allocations for Elementary and Secondary Schools*. Ann Arbor, MI: University of Michigan, 1979.

Klotman, Robert H. *The School Music Administrator and Supervisor*. Englewood Cliffs, NJ: Prentice-Hall, 1973.

Knudsen, V.O., and C.M. Harris. *Acoustical Designing in Architecture*. New York: John Wiley and Sons, 1950.

Lonnbury, Warren C. *Theatre Backstage from A to Z*. Seattle and London: University of Washington Press, 1967.

Meske, Eunice Boardman, and Carroll Rinehart. *Individualized Instruction in Music*. Reston, VA: MENC, 1975.

Music Educators National Conference. *The School Music Program: Description and Standards*. Reston, VA: MENC, 1986.

Noise Control: Principles and Practice. Marlborough, MA: Bruel and Kjaer Instruments, 1982.

Parker, W. Oren, and Harvey K. Smith. *Scene Design and Stage Lighting*. 3d ed. New York: Holt, Rinehart and Winston, 1973.

Rettinger, Michael. *Acoustic Design and Noise Control*. New York: Chemical Publishing, 1977.

Robinson, Horace. *Architecture for Educational Theatre*. Eugene: University of Oregon Press, 1971.

Talaske, Richard H., Ewart A. Wetherill, and William J. Cavanaugh. *Halls for Music Performance: Two Decades of Experience, 1962–1982*. New York: American Institute of Physics, 1982.

Trythall, Gilbert. *Principles and Practices of Electronic Music*. New York: Grosset and Dunlap, 1973.

Yerges, Lyle F. *Sound, Noise, and Vibration Control*. New York: Van Nostrand Reinhold, 1969.

ARTICLES

Braun, William. "Find It Fast With a Music Library Data Base." *Music Educators Journal* 73, no. 7, March 1987, 52.

Geerdes, Harold P. "Acoustics for the Music Educator." *The School Musician*, March 1974, 44.

Geerdes, Harold P. "Adjustable Acoustics in Music Performance." *Music Educators Journal* 61, no. 8. April 1975, 40.

Ingebretsen, Robert B. "Personal Computers: Introduction and Software." *Sound and Video Contractor* 2, no. 4, April 1985.

Klepper, David L., William J. Cavanaugh, and L. Gerald Marshall. "Noise Control in Music Teaching Facilities." *Noise Control Engineering* 15, no. 2, September/October 1980.

Lewer, Mark, "A User's Guide to MIDI." *Recording Engineer/Producer* 17, no. 3, June 1986.

Magrill, Samuel. "Synthesizer Ensembles: An Idea for the Eighties." *The Instrumentalist* 41, no. 11, June 1987, 32–38.

Mahin, Bruce P. "Choosing a Computer." *The Instrumentalist* 41, no. 11, June 1987, 23–31.

Music Educators National Conference. "Computers and Music Education." *Music Educators Journal* 73, no. 4, December 1986.

"Music, Midi, and Manufacturers." *The Instrumentalist*, June 1987, 67–71.

BOOKLETS

Acoustical and Insulating Materials Association. *Performance Data on Architectural Acoustical Materials*. Park Ridge, IL: AIMA, 1973.

Acoustical and Insulating Materials Association. *The Use of Architectural Acoustical Materials: Theory and Practice*. Park Ridge, IL: AIMA, 1972.

City of New York. *Building Code: Local Law No. 76 of the City of New York*. New York: The City Record, 1968.

United States Gypsum Company. *Sound Control Construction*. Chicago: USGC, 1972.

Wenger Corporation. *Performing Area Acoustics*. Owatonna, MN: Wenger, 1985.

MUSIC SOFTWARE CATALOGS AND COMPANIES

Coda
Wenger Corporation
1401 East Seventy-ninth Street
Bloomington, MN 55420

Music Education Solutions
Temporal Acuity Products
300–120th Avenue, NE
Bellevue, WA 98005

Music Instruction Software
Electronic Courseware Systems
1210 Lancaster Drive
Champaign, IL 61821

Maestro Music
2403 San Mateo NE, Suite P-6
Albuquerque, NM 87110

Minnesota Educational Computing Corporation
3490 Lexington Avenue
St. Paul, MN 55212

RolandCorp US
7200 Dominion Circle
Los Angeles, CA 90040

COMMON ACOUSTICAL PROBLEMS

Problem	Cause	Remedy
Poor sound isolation	Wrong type of construction Sound leaks between spaces Sound finds a flanking path Ventilating system carries sound	Seating of cement block, adding resilient skins to wall, caulking fine cracks, stuffing openings around pipes or outlet boxes with fiber glass, adding absorption in the room to cut down volume at the source Deliberate introduction of some noise into the air-handling system can help mask intruding sounds, if done carefully
Noisy ventilating system	Too high volume of air moving at too high speed Vibrations being transmitted Lack of care in design or installation	Change pulleys to slow down fan and air movement Replace conventional ducts with lined ductwork Install special grilles Vibration at the source can be curtailed by using resilient hangers on equipment, and isolation joints in ducts and pipes
Muddled sound in a "live" rehearsal room or hall.	Too many hard, reflective surfaces Parallel walls Absence of nearby reflectors	Destroy parallelism by adding a new interior wall on two sides Add absorption to the offending surfaces: tile, drapes, tectum If floor and ceiling are parallel, carpet the floor or add acoustical ceiling tile
Poor balance or blend	Ceiling too low Absence of nearby reflectors Heavy draperies on stage; a live auditorium	No remedy for a low ceiling Add hard surfaces near ensemble Remove draperies or install a reflective acoustical shell
Dead and lifeless tone	Too little volume in the room Excessive absorption Too low a ceiling	No remedy for smallness or space or low ceiling in existing rooms Sealing block or tile and removing heavy drapes and/or carpeting
Live and jumbled tone, lacking in clarity	Poor room shaping Excessive reflective surfaces	Shape properly with new interior walls or closets and cabinets Carefully add absorption
Boomy and over-resonant sound	Space is too large (excessive volume) Lack of low-frequency absorption Parallel walls and parallel floor and ceiling	Add sound reflecting panels Add low-frequency absorbers Carefully add absorption to some surfaces
Can't hear on stage	Heavy velour draperies High fly space, filled with "dirty linen" Absence of nearby reflectors	Remove draperies for music concerts Install an acoustical shell

INDEX

C   50

1034-02-2M-11/87
1034-10-2M-5/89